GAME ON

BIANCA CHATFIELD & LEIGH RUSSELL

hardie grant books

contents

INTRODUCTION

Have you thought about where you are heading and how you are going to get there? Are you dreaming big – and then playing big? Or have you kept it safe, but know you are capable of more? Perhaps you have not given much thought at all to what you genuinely want out of life?

It's time to start living the life you've always wanted and being the person you've always wanted to be. And to get different results, you need to start thinking differently. Do what you are capable of – and more. We know one thing for certain from our combined experiences: people are ALWAYS more capable than they realise or give themselves credit for. It's time to consider whether your personal and professional habits are like a team of cheerleaders on the sidelines, egging you on, or like a group of negative Nellys hindering your success.

We started our business together, The Ignition Project, to work with women to redefine their version of success and coach them to be the best they can be. Why? Because everywhere we go, no matter what the industry, women sell themselves short; don't believe in what they are truly capable of; or are unaware of how to develop a game plan to bring their dreams to life. We frequently hear about the gaps, the areas that still need work, and previous mistakes and failings. Even worse, some women hold onto imagined future failings that force them to jog on the spot, rather than get out there and build the career and life they really want.

Can you relate to that? Are you nodding and agreeing as you read this? Then sit back, relax and grab a cuppa, because we can't wait to work with you. Just imagine the impact if every woman you know (including YOU) translated her dreams into reality – even those dreams that had only been whispered to her besties or not at all. It would be incredible.

The traditional notions of what a career is made up of and women's status in the workplace have been turned on their head in the last few decades. The game has changed and we are only at the tip of the iceberg in terms of seeing what is possible. What an exciting time to be alive!

SPORT AND WHY IT DOESN'T MATTER IF IT'S NOT YOUR THING

A huge part of our professional and personal lives has been spent in elite sport and the business of leadership. We have come to understand, through our successes and failures, that there are no shortcuts to achieving our dreams, no matter what society and the media tells us. Sport has taught us that we need to formulate a great strategy to make sure we are in the game and give everything we have once the game is on. Go hard or go home. It has taught us to live in a way that gets the best out of ourselves, the people around us and the communities we serve.

Sport is one of the passions we both share. But *Game On* is so much more than a book about sport. In all honesty (and you will learn that we like to be upfront), don't shut this book because sport isn't exactly your 'thing'. It actually doesn't matter – not one little bit. Sure, sport is the platform we use to share our learnings, failures and successes, but what we really care about is much bigger than sport itself. For both of us, it has always been about personal excellence and supporting, challenging and inspiring others to be the best they can be.

This book is the product of our passion and expertise. Our collective experience has taken many forms, including professional athlete, secondary teacher, leadership coach, executive, CEO, public speaker and facilitator. We've created our own businesses and executed the vision. Now, we are business partners and spend our time dreaming up even bigger and bolder ways to impact the world. We are endlessly fascinated with how to foster high performance and are committed to being the best versions of ourselves we can be while soaking up as much information, theory and best practice as possible from around the world. We have been surrounded by the best of the best for a long time, working with many top performers, and we know what these people do better than anyone else. We know how they get their game on. And we hope to inspire you to be your best self and bring out the best in your team — whatever kind of team that might be.

The pressure cooker of high-performance sporting environments brings out the best and worst in people, and being smart and savvy is essential to sustaining top levels of performance. *Game On* brings these strategies together to coach you to achieve personal excellence, whatever your passion, whether you need to get your game on, stay in the game or get ahead of the game. You are not taught these things growing up, so we are here to show you how to not only survive in the world of work and leadership, but to thrive. Mechanics are easy. Dynamics? Not so much.

CHANGE IS SLOW ... BUT WORTH IT

People love to talk about success as an isolated event, as something that just *happens*. It's not as sexy to think of success as merely a series of moments, but it is exactly that; it's the sum of all our choices.

The fact that you have picked up this book suggests you are curious to learn more and do more. Perhaps you have already made a decision to start putting some time and effort into yourself? We think that is a great decision, but we have a word of caution: it's tough and unrealistic to make huge or dramatic changes quickly. Like losing weight, real change can't be achieved after one day of eating well (we only wish that were the case). The reality is that long-lasting change and great success is about making small adjustments, learning along the way and putting yourself out there. We are going to throw a whole lot of stuff at you and, as you work through it with us, we want you to figure out what is best for you.

And while we aim to inspire you, we also have another equally important aim: we don't want to fill your head with any palaver. For us, there is a big difference between inspirational 'you can do it' quotes and advice that is grounded. You're a smart chick, so you are resourceful enough to read theory books if you want to. But we figure that what you really need, particularly in this busy, modern life, is a book that gets to the heart of it, a companion that you can call on when you need a bit of coaching, a touch of sparkle, or a practical idea for how to make change happen. **We are your women and *Game On* is the new ace up your sleeve.**

We care about YOU, YOUR journey and YOUR version of success. But, most importantly, we care about giving you tools, tricks and tips to help you nail the kind of career and life you want.

HOW TO USE THIS BOOK

We have written *Game On* so you can use it the way you need or want to: read from start to finish, or pick a section you really want to focus on. Most importantly, treat *Game On* like a coach that sits on your bedside table. Come back to it when you need a fresh perspective, a reminder, a pep talk, or when you need to focus on a particular area.

Before you dive in, know this: we want you to explore who you are, what path you might take and how you are going to ignite your game. We won't pretend this stuff is easy. It's not, but it's important. Or in other words, it's totally worth your time and energy. It's an investment in you and your future self. But, like everything, you only get out what you put in. We need you to do the work. If you pick up this book and only read, you will have been on only part of the journey. Don't waste your time. You have to *do* something. #GameOn women have no time for complacency.

Throughout the book, we share some of our stories and reflections, and at the end of each chapter there are ideas and questions to contemplate and tasks for you to try. Go into this with a curious, open mind and we promise it will have an impact.

We talk a lot about creating a great game plan. We truly believe that you will be more successful if you do some planning, reflect on what you genuinely want to aim for, then make sure you know what to do when you hit speed bumps (and you will). *Game On* is divided into five parts that represent key areas to work through when creating your own game plan for success.

So, are you ready to get your game on? Let's begin.

WHO ARE THESE

TWO CHICKS?

LEIGH ON BIANCA ...

The first (and most obvious) thing to know about Bianca is that she is tall. So tall in fact that when you walk with her through a crowd, people can't help but stare. She has such grace though that she just smiles, making people feel instantly comfortable around her. The second and most significant thing is that she is a rare human who knows what it takes to be successful and not only talks the talk, but walks the walk.

Bianca is most recognised for her incredible elite sporting achievements in netball – she is a Commonwealth Games Gold and Silver medallist, a World Champion and played over 240 games for the Melbourne Phoenix and Melbourne Vixens. She captained at both clubs and won six premierships in total. At the age of eighteen, when all her other mates were just starting to go out and enjoy the things teenagers do, Bianca was representing Australia. She was determined and driven from the get-go and hasn't stopped or slowed down since.

But that is just the start of her life of purpose. She is a qualified teacher and also has grad qualifications in management and elite athlete mentoring. She has successfully started up two businesses (The Ignition Project and Pivot Performance), has created an elite netball academy to support aspiring athletes, regularly appears on radio and TV, and is frequently asked to speak on a range of topics at schools, sporting groups and corporate events.

She is passionate about leadership, women in sport, living a healthy lifestyle and getting the message about what it takes to achieve high performance out to as many people as possible.

Behind the scenes, Bianca loves her exercise, has an obsession with the latest beauty products, is a skilled self-tanner and makes awful green smoothies that she loves to pretend are great. (I don't care how good they are for you, they are truly terrible.)

BIANCA ON LEIGH …

Leigh has a kick-arse, supercharged approach to life. I was in awe of her, and maybe a little intimidated by her, when we first met in 2008 (don't tell her that).

She is a straight talking, creative, no-nonsense kind of chick, but manages to do it all with such care and compassion. She is passionate about women in sport and business, and is forever pushing others outside of their comfort zones. If you ever doubt yourself, she'll set you straight before you even understand what's going on. One of Leigh's coaching clients described her as 'a pleasant punch in the face'. I couldn't have said it better myself!

Her résumé is chock-full of experience, from qualifications in the arts, teaching, counselling and management, to a CEO position at Netball Victoria and directorships of various companies. Her latest endeavours really do tap her passion and have taken her into the entrepreneurial world. She has two businesses (Inspired Heads and The Ignition Project), presents 'Ahead of the Game' workshops and has a role in Foxtel's *The Recruit* as Mind Coach.

And just to make us feel even more inadequate, she is a wife (a footy WAG of sorts – she'll kill me for saying that), a mum to three kids and manages her career and family life with ease, like no-one I have ever seen before.

Please don't be fooled by this image of perfection though. She does have tendencies to be severely impatient, is often frustrated by simply using a computer and has a love–hate relationship with the world of social media, which I'm slowly getting her to embrace. Give her a follow @leighmrussell and help me out.

GETTING
YOUR

game On

creating a strong foundation for success

We all have dreams and goals we would like to achieve in life, from personal ones, like getting fit or running a marathon, to career goals like being financially secure or landing a dream job. Being unclear about direction can lead to self-doubt, a lack of motivation, worry and stress, which can cause us to give up. Every savvy chick needs a great plan.

But hold it right there. There is no point having a lofty dream but a shaky foundation. Top performers make sure that all the 'little big things' – those seemingly small factors that, put together, make a powerful contribution to their chances of success – are in place. Getting your game on requires you to pay attention to these factors and build your success from the ground up. So before we worry about the end product, let's work through how to get your game on. Let's talk about the things that really matter in your career and life – all the things that will help you to be the best you can be.

> Great players specialise in the basics - they take the common disciplines of the game to an uncommon level.
>
> – BIANCA AND LEIGH

CHAPTER 1
DREAMING OF SUCCESS? GET TO WORK

Straight up, we want to get you thinking about the concept of success. Your success. You see, a lot of time, energy and even suffering are caught up in misconceptions of what success really is. We all know someone who is successful by traditional standards but is otherwise completely miserable. To avoid this trap, you want to be sure of what you are chasing before you start, otherwise when you get there, it may not *feel* successful. Have you really thought about your version of success? And what it will take to achieve it?

Don't let others (or the media) define what success means for you. The traditional vision of success – fame, money, power – has had its day in the sun. There are countless ways to define success, so you may need to rethink the definition you have in your head.

Success is such a personal thing because, of course, we are all built differently. For us, it means achieving life goals, making a contribution and a difference to people. A successful life is about making sure we reach our potential and strive for personal excellence in everything we do.

What is it for you? What is most important to you? What are you truly passionate about? Success is only meaningful if it connects with *your* inner purpose and passion. Are you living that way, or are you fudging around with stuff that isn't going to get you there? There is one absolute truth about success — you will never get it if you are looking in the wrong places.

We mention this now, because we don't want you to get to the end of the book not having thought about it. We want to work with YOU and YOUR dreams from the beginning. The only way to move forward is to get clear, then get going.

THE SECRET OF SUCCESS

#shinysuccess Success that seems remarkable, straightforward or easy

It's time to tell you the real truth about success: there *is* no secret, so don't let anyone tell you otherwise. Tales of #shinysuccess make us feel like we could never do the same. But, more often than not, the interesting, juicy and helpful detail has been left out: the days where it was hard and the moments where it would have been easier to give up. It's easy to forget the tough times when you've made it to the other side. People have a special knack for forgetting just how challenging an experience was and like to tell themselves they have tapped into some magic force, instead of acknowledging their success actually involved a whole lot of hard work.

Being successful is a journey that involves ups and downs, false starts, mistakes and a load of hard graft. That's why you have to be sure of your goals, so the tough times are worth it. If it means enough to you, you will be able to sustain it. If you are working towards someone else's version of success, the slog will be harder than it has to be.

> Success is liking yourself,
> liking what you do and
> liking how you do it.
> – MAYA ANGELOU

MAKE TINY ADJUSTMENTS FOR A BIG RESULT

Being successful isn't some magic formula; it is about adopting positive habits that you practice over and over again. It isn't about the big, audacious actions, but more about the sum of all the little actions.

This success strategy became well known in elite sport after the amazing performance of the British cycling team over a few short years. In the late 1990s and early 2000s, the British cycling team was not seen as a true competitor in any of the major competitions. But the then Director of Performance and current manager of Team Sky, Sir David Brailsford, changed all that when he implemented the 'marginal gains' philosophy. Within a few short years of adopting this strategy, Team Sky had won the Tour de France three times (in 2012, 2013 and 2015).

So, what did he do? Instead of making major changes, David decided it was the aggregation of marginal gains that would make the difference. Or, in other words, the team defined the goal then worked backwards to set smaller goals, identifying all the little big things that would add up to success. For David Brailsford and his team, this meant breaking down and identifying every tiny aspect of performance for the athletes, and then making just a one per cent improvement in every area. They left no stone unturned — the team famously would even take their own mattresses to hotels they were staying at, such was their belief that the tiny things mattered. The result? Their overall performance was significantly enhanced.

You don't have to be an elite cyclist to adopt this success strategy. You simply need to move towards your goal by making tiny daily adjustments, then repeating them over and over.

Almost every habit you have leads you towards success or away from it. And of course, these habits are the result of many small decisions over time. We forget this too often and convince ourselves that change is only meaningful if it is big. Take the example of trying to lose weight. The usual thing to do is to *go* on a diet, which usually means making drastic changes to the way you eat. But how long does that change actually last? You have a greater chance of success if you make tiny adjustments to your lifestyle each day, over and over, and keep doing it. And, happily, small changes are easier to make than drastic changes. Win-win, game on!

Bianca's Story

I was 19 when I went to the 2002 Manchester Commonwealth Games as a Reserve (so not really part of the team, but a training partner in case of injury). The girls won the gold medal in double overtime and I remember watching and thinking to myself that winning a gold medal for Australia at the Commonwealth Games would be the pinnacle of my career.

Throughout most of my time in the Diamonds squad (2000–2014) that gold medal was quite elusive. The last time we'd had a win was in 2002, so in the lead-up to 2014 we were on a serious mission to change the momentum. We needed to significantly review how we went about things, and not just concentrate on the end result. Our main rivals, New Zealand, weren't lucky to have won the gold in 2006 and 2010, they had been in prime condition at the right time.

As athletes, we put so much pressure on ourselves and expect every change that we make to give us earth-shattering results. I was annoyingly always questioning my strength and conditioning coaches about my programs; I wanted them to perform miracles in a week (totally unrealistic, I know).

I watched a documentary about the British cycling team that explained how they had used the marginal gains philosophy in their training to change the culture and success of the team. I was so inspired by this way of thinking that it became the way I approached my preparation on and off the court, and with the team.

After the Diamonds' 2010 loss, we spent three years changing habits: the way we trained, the type of training we did and the way we recovered. We spent more time on monitoring players individually, our communication and knowing our sleep patterns. We concentrated on how we lived and ate on tour, and how we gave each other feedback, and the list goes on.

For us, changing the small things wasn't noticeable, or noticeable at first, but in the end it helped us get to the Commonwealth Games in great condition. We knew we had done everything in the lead-up, and that no matter who showed up to play us on court, we could win. We won the final by 18 goals. It wasn't luck on our side – ticking off all those little changes along the way had given us confidence in each other and the belief that all that hard work would get us the result we wanted.

be your best self

What is important to you when it comes to your success? What does it look like for you? If that is a hard starting point, think about the times when you have been most proud. Imagine you're at the end of your life and write a list of your achievements.

The harder you work the LUCKIER YOU get.

WINNING PLAYS

- MAKE SURE YOU ARE CHASING THE RIGHT KIND OF SUCCESS (THE ONLY KIND): YOUR VERSION.

- GET CLEAR ON WHAT YOU WANT TO ACHIEVE AND FOCUS ON.

- THERE IS NO SECRET TO SUCCESS, YOU HAVE TO 'TAKE THE STAIRS'.

- TINY ADJUSTMENTS TRUMP BIG CHANGES.

- EVERY HABIT YOU HAVE LEADS YOU TOWARDS SUCCESS (OR AWAY FROM IT).

CHAPTER 2

CHOOSE YOUR MINDSET, CREATE YOUR WORLD

Mindset is everything

We often go in search of complicated strategies to unlock our true potential, but, as it turns out, our most powerful tool hovers just above our shoulders: our brain. It's what we *decide* to do with it that makes a difference. The kind of mindset you have, the way you treat your body and the way you use your mind and body together will determine how life pans out for you.

TOP PERFORMERS USE THEIR HEADS

Mental models

Mental models act as filters in our understanding of how the world works and reveal why we make the choices we do. We all have unique ideas and behaviours because we are all running the information we receive through different mental models (which are made up of our values, assumptions, beliefs and experiences). They inform our ideas about how things work. And once you have an internal thought process (or mental model) about how something works, it shapes your behaviour.

We sometimes think we can't control what type of mental model is used in different situations. **But we do have a choice.**

What runs through your mind? What are some of the things you often say to yourself? What are your beliefs, fears and assumptions? Chances are these thoughts make up your current mental models. How do your thoughts translate into behaviours? Are they helping or hindering?

Paying attention to the choices you make is a vitally important success strategy. It is the difference between achieving your goals or not. Mental models matter; they define how willing you are to try new things, how you plan, how you deal with speed bumps and how creative you are in accomplishing what is important to you.

Using a high-performance mindset

There are plenty of naturally talented people out there, but few are willing to do the work to maximise their *whole* talent. Athletes with long and successful sporting careers don't rely on their talent alone. They may make it look easy, but it rarely ever is. **If it were easy, everyone would do it!** Successful athletes decide to use their mindsets to their advantage. It's as simple as that.

To be a #GameOn kind of woman, you need to use a high-performance mindset – one that means you believe in your own power and capacity to learn, change and

> You become what you think. So make sure you are telling yourself the right things often.
>
> – BIANCA AND LEIGH

nail the things you want to achieve. Using a high-performance mindset allows you to maximise your capabilities and, most importantly, capitalise on the opportunities that come your way. Notice we said you have to *use* a high-performance mindset, not *have* a high-performance mindset. It comes back to this thing about choice. You decide to use it or not. The views you choose to adopt about your career, leadership and life profoundly impact your experience and ability to achieve the things you want.

When life throws you curve balls, your choices will be tested. Paying attention to the little big things when it comes to mindset is like a gift you give yourself to help you cope with different situations (and it just keeps on giving).

THE GRATITUDE ATTITUDE

It's too easy to focus on the stuff that hasn't happened yet, or didn't go so well. It takes more effort to be consistently positive and – more than that – grateful for what you have and the opportunities in front of you. And guess what? Your gratitude attitude, or lack of it, has a huge impact on others (who then have an impact on you).

So what is gratitude? It's about appreciating what you have, not what you don't. Don't worry – we haven't gone all soft on you. Being grateful is a genuine high-performance strategy. It's about shifting your focus from the problems with something to all the possible solutions and outcomes. Doesn't that sound worth adopting?

Bianca's Story

When Lisa Alexander started coaching the Diamonds she instituted a tradition when she gave us all a journal at the beginning of her first tour. From then on she would hand them out to each player with the understanding we would use it in some way.

At first, I wasn't that excited by this concept, but some girls wrote daily journals and others used it as an organiser or for general notes, to draw pictures or work game analysis.

For me, it was initially just the notebook that I used for all sorts of things, from scribbling down people's details, to planning my next presentation.

In 2013, when I was coming to the end of my career, it was always a struggle to keep fit, and I found myself spending a lot more time on my own, having to do extras for recovery, such as ice baths. Often, I would be in a fairly negative headspace when I was having ice baths on my own. I would always try and be positive in front of the team, but as soon as I was on my own in the ice bath I felt frustrated by my situation.

My emotions were easier to deal with when I was at home in Melbourne and had time to myself, but when on tour with the Aussie team, I refused to be that negative, whinging person that brought down the vibe of the group. So I thought the best use for the journal would be to follow one of my teammates and use it as a gratitude journal.

I would be lying if I said I wrote in it every day, but I did try to make time every few days. One of my teammates, Sharni Layton, and I would also make a point of texting each other 'gratitude moments' when we had an amazing experience or just a day where we felt lucky to be doing what we were doing. I loved the fact that we would keep each other accountable. Making time for this really helped me to maintain a positive mindset throughout the tournament and cope with everything that was mentally and physically challenging at the end of my playing career. It was such a simple, but powerful, strategy that I wish I had used it from the very start of my career.

Having a gratitude attitude is a way of life. Choosing the direction of your thoughts is always something that is in your control. Control your thoughts or they end up controlling you.

THE POWER OF SOCIAL MEDIA

Social media can have a huge influence on your mindset. When you scroll through all the positive images and quotes on Instagram or Facebook, everything you see will evoke some kind reaction. Some of that stuff is awesome. But there is an uncomfortable truth that no-one really wants to admit: social media is a vehicle that allows us to show the best bits of our lives and tell our #shinysuccess stories. Hardly anyone (including us) puts up bad photos of themselves on social media. The impact? You end up comparing your everyday to someone else's highlight reel.

No matter what you see, hear or read, it's important to keep your thoughts in check and refocus their direction if you need to, because your thoughts are the root of everything.

MAKE HAPPINESS A CHOICE

When you first wake up in the morning, your thoughts can go one of two ways: you either think about all the things you don't want to do that day, and the things that could potentially go wrong, or you think about the good things that you are looking forward to, and how to use the day to move towards your future self.

But stop right there. We know what you are thinking. *It's not easy to wake up every day and choose my mindset.* We totally agree. *It's easy for other people but not me.* Right? Wrong.

I am not what happened
to me. I am what I choose
to become.

– CARL JUNG

We won't pretend it's easy to always look at the positive side of everything. Sometimes life deals up difficult situations and our gratitude attitude can be tested. But coping well with the hard, challenging days becomes easier when you realise you have a choice in what you focus on. And if you fall off the positivity bandwagon, you can get right back on it. A bad day doesn't have to mean a bad week, which can turn into a bad month or even a bad year. The key is to identify when your mind has drifted into a negative pattern and when you need to bring the focus back to positive thoughts. Positivity doesn't happen to you, you've gotta make it happen.

RESILIENCE

There are a few things that are perceived as must-haves for elite performers in sport, such as freakish genetics, an incredible physique, mental toughness and the attributes of a perfect role model. They are expected to build relationships with the media, fans, sponsors and teammates. Resilience is also seen as an essential trait for athletes.

Resilience is hard to define and equally tough to measure. So let's keep our definition simple: it's how you get up after getting knocked down, it's how you deal with surprises, and how you utilise your in-built shock absorbers to adapt to change.

Chances are, you have it on board already. Been through a tough time or some sort of adversity and gotten through it? You have shown resilience. Resilience truly defines your character by shaping the way you react to difficult situations. Make resilience part of your mindset to get the best out of yourself each day.

Bianca's Story

I think of my whole Diamonds career as one long roller-coaster ride. Don't get me wrong, there were plenty of highlights and amazing times, but behind the scenes it was always a battle.

The most challenging part of my netball career was being dropped from the Diamonds in 2010 in the lead-up to the Commonwealth Games in India.

Selections for the Delhi Commonwealth Games were held at the Australian Institute of Sport (AIS) and, although the facilities are great, it was not generally my favourite place to go. The process is fairly gruelling; after five days of being tested in every way possible, the selectors choose a final team of 12. The process was to inform us of the selections with the staff, coaches and players together in one room. They read out the team of 12 in alphabetical order. If your name was read out, you stayed and awkwardly congratulated one another. If you weren't in the team, things were a lot tougher. It was a bit like being on the reality TV show, *Survivor*. You stood up and walked out with everyone staring at you, headed back to your room, packed your bag and made your own way to the airport.

That particular year, when I had to walk the plank, there was no welfare support or team psychologist to talk to. In fact, everyone seemed too scared to speak to me. I made my way to the airport and had two hours to kill. Those two hours, as I came to terms with my new reality, were tough. I ended up leaving the airport and going for a walk to avoid speaking to anyone. I was trying to cope with a gamut of emotions. I was embarrassed, upset with the feedback they had given me and angry because the opportunity to compete in the Commonwealth Games only came around every four years. How could I possibly be around for another four years knowing how exhausting it was trying to stay in the team, let alone shine amongst the young defenders who had taken over? On the other hand, I was relieved, in a way, that I finally had a break, albeit a forced one.

I hadn't been in this position for a long time, and it was tough. I had to work through it bit by bit and the only way I really got through was by having some awesome people around me, people who didn't just feel sorry for me. Sure, they had empathy towards my situation, but what helped the most was that they gave me productive things to do and think about that ultimately helped me get back on track. A former coach and mentor (and legend of netball), Joyce Brown was one person who helped. She knew I was hurting and she knew how to get me to see things differently. This is one of the many gifts she shares with lots of us athletes.

At the time, this experience was a gift in disguise. It made me reassess everything, look at my career outside of playing sport and make some tough decisions. I took some time out to rest my body both physically and mentally, learned to suck it up, move forward and do something with my life that was more meaningful and rewarding than just focusing on myself as an athlete. It sparked my passion for player welfare, too. Once I was back on the team, I worked closely with the Diamonds to make sure we had enough support resources around the players.

Ultimately, it taught me that I was in complete control of my mindset. No matter what happened, I had it within me to cope. The mind is a powerful tool; control what you can and if you can't, then let it go. I'd often heard Leigh say that 90 per cent of your performance happens above your shoulders. It's only now that I completely understand that.

> Success is a few simple disciplines, practised every day; while failure is simply a few errors in judgement, repeated every day.
>
> – JIM ROHN

SUPERWOMAN IS A FICTIONAL CHARACTER

Let's get one thing straight. It's totally OK to show your vulnerabilities and to admit you are having a bad day, but it's the way you *handle* it that is most important.

You don't have to have it together all the time, and doing it alone isn't necessarily a sign of strength. Modern-day superwoman is able to be authentic about how she is travelling, and ask for help from others now and then.

Think about a challenging time in your life when you had to front up to work even though you wished you could have curled up in bed and stayed there. How did you handle it? How did you get through the day? What could you have done differently?

GETTING LUCKY

We all have a friend who we think is 'lucky'. We hear about lucky people a lot. They seem to have a special superpower we don't have that makes good things happen. If only we were as lucky as they are, then we too could achieve great things.

In elite sport, there is an element of luck involved in being successful (for example, not falling over someone's leg at a precise moment). But seriously, hardly any of those things are to do with luck. Most of it is down to hard work and paying attention to the little things, day after day, month after month.

Wasting time comparing ourselves to others is all too common and we need to cut it out. All of us. (See p. 87 for more.) When we compare ourselves to others, we convince ourselves that others have what they want because they got 'lucky'. Having this mindset absolves us from taking responsibility for our own lives. How can you enjoy your achievements if you think it is luck that got you there?

Lucky people aren't blessed because some magical being in the universe is granting them wishes. They work hard, try again, work harder, and move forward, until they get the result they want. Perseverance is not as sexy as luck, but it's a much better long-term success strategy. Save your luck for your lottery ticket.

be your best self

Write a gratitude journal (you can also download a gratitude journal app) by recording your moments of gratitude daily, at least for a couple of weeks. Or you might want to enlist a friend and text each other your moments of gratitude at the end of the day.

A number of studies have demonstrated that a variety of positive benefits can come from using a gratitude journal (or something similar), including the possibility of rewiring your brain – absolutely amazing! After you have kept track of your moments of gratitude for at least a couple of weeks, analyse the impact keeping the journal has had on you.

To do this, ask yourself, has this journal changed anything for me? Do I feel happier and calmer, and am I more focused on my haves, rather than my have-nots?

Look back at what you have written. Are there themes? Is there anything surprising? Rather than just tallying up all the good things, think about what your life might be like without the people, things and events you are grateful for.

Most importantly, don't analyse your spelling and grammar, or criticise the format of your journal. Whether it's a few scraps of paper or a fancy notebook, there is no right way to create a gratitude journal.

THOUGHTS MANIFEST AS WORDS

WORDS TURN INTO ACTIONS

ACTIONS DEVELOP INTO HABITS

HABITS HARDEN INTO CHARACTER

WINNING PLAYS

- USE WHAT YOU HAVE ABOVE YOUR SHOULDERS WISELY AND YOU WILL AUTOMATICALLY BE IN FRONT.

- YOU ARE WHAT YOU THINK, SO CHOOSE MINDFULLY.

- ADOPT A GRATITUDE ATTITUDE AS A WAY OF LIFE, RATHER THAN AN ISOLATED ACT.

- RESILIENCE IS A GAME CHANGER.

- LUCK IS OVERRATED. HOPE IS NOT A STRATEGY.

CHAPTER 3
EMOTIONAL FITNESS

Be fit enough — mentally and physically — to face the world head on.

Emotional fitness is absolutely essential in kicking career and life goals, but it isn't the first thing that often comes to mind when talking about your career, your life, or even fitness itself. We are all familiar with the benefits of physical fitness, but to give yourself the best possible chance of achieving your aspirations, mental fitness should also be a top priority. And, like anything, it takes work.

Emotional fitness is about having a strong and healthy mind that allows you to tackle the challenges you face and make the most of opportunities that come your way.

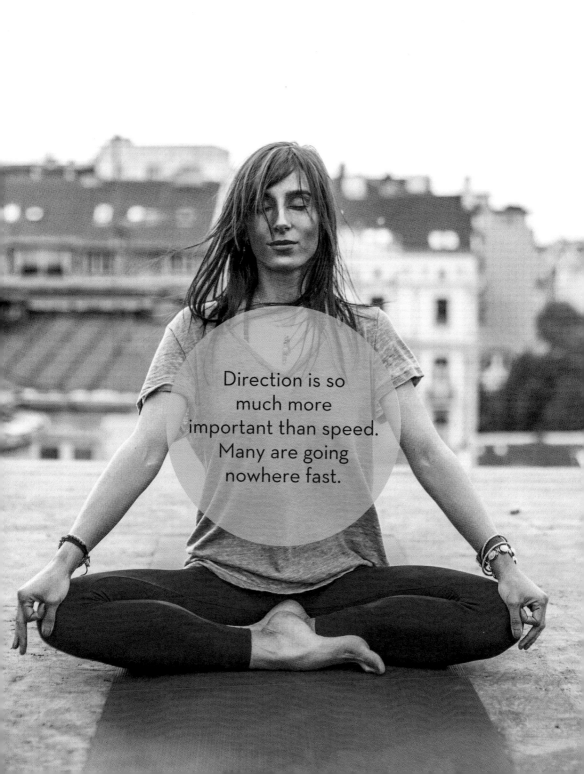

Direction is so much more important than speed. Many are going nowhere fast.

The brain is a muscle; if you don't look after it and give it a regular workout, it loses tone. Mental fitness is a journey that requires you to take responsibility for yourself; make sure you are able to thrive, not simply survive.

EMOTIONAL FITNESS STARTS WITH YOUR MOST IMPORTANT RELATIONSHIP

The most important relationship you have is the one you have with yourself. Taking care of yourself, mentally and physically, is not selfish. In fact, making your wellness a top priority means you can do more and give more! It helps to make you a better leader, friend, sister and daughter. We are not flippantly suggesting that this is easy, but it is definitely important. Why do airlines ask you to put on your oxygen mask before trying to help anyone else? It's because without your own line of oxygen, you are no good to anyone. The same applies to your life.

But sometimes, taking care of yourself seems to come way down the priority list. The demands on our time and capabilities often far exceed our capacity. Being constantly active has become the norm, but contradicts what we know about the brain and the body, and how they work together for high performance.

THE CONCEPT OF BALANCE AND WHY IT ISN'T HELPFUL

The term work–life balance is one we have come to dislike for a very simple reason: it implies that there is a utopian level of balance to which we should all aspire (and then of course, feel bad when we can't get there). Work–life balance only becomes an issue when you don't like what you are doing for work or you have not been able to say no to competing demands.

Balance is all about perspective. What is balance for one might be out of whack for another. Looking for an easy way to work it out? If you feel like you are a rubber band that is about to snap, you are out of balance.

Instead of talking about balance, we should be thinking about energy and how to sustain our performance, and the personal strategies we use to make things happen.

Leigh's story

The balance between motherhood and work has been full of ups and downs for me, like I imagine it is for everyone. I was 27 when I had my first baby, 35 my last, and I have tried a range of different working arrangements, including 15 months' maternity leave, being back at work after six weeks, part-time work, full-time work and running my own businesses. This makes me an expert at my life, not yours, but I hope what I have learned might help you on your journey. We don't talk about this stuff enough, preferring to focus on judging rather than supporting each other in this crazy intersection between the personal and professional.

Here is what I have learned about work and motherhood:

- You can love your kids insanely and still love your career. The two are not mutually exclusive. Never apologise for wanting both to be part of your life.

- Never apologise for being a mother. It is part of what you bring to the table. I have never heard a dad apologise for being a father.

- Never apologise for being home with the kids. 'I'm just a stay-at-home mum'. We all know how hard that job is. Be proud of whatever decision you make. Drop the word 'just' in that sentence.

- There is never a right time to have a child. New job, young age, promotion, whatever. Just do what you want to do and trust that things will work out.

- The concept of a one-size-fits-all balance is unhelpful. In fact, it just makes you feel guilty all the time. Family needs are constantly changing, so define your own sense of balance.

- Drop trying to be a perfect mother and stop listening to everyone else about how to do it all. Self-acceptance is such a powerful thing. When I accepted myself, I became a better mother and happier at work.

- The ability to laugh at yourself and the messiness of life is also helpful. That, and crying. Whatever works on any given day.

- Being a mother made me a better professional. I quickly learned to manage my time better, not sweat the small stuff and get super focused.

- Most days are chaotic but that is not particular to motherhood. That's just life. No job fits in between nine and five, and most come with multiple responsibilities. Success means hard work, kids or not.

- You are going to miss out on things with the kids, but that is totally fine. Kids are great at giving you the puppy-dog face, but they don't need you there for every school event. Get to the ones you can and let go of the ones you can't. Schools, like many workplaces, are not set up for working parents.

- You might miss out on some things at work, but that is also totally fine. Get to the things that are crucial and let go of the rest. Focus on building strong relationships rather than ticking every box.

- If you are working part-time, work part-time. Don't get paid for three days and work for five. Your employer is not doing you a favour by giving you a job or allowing you to work from home.

- You will know when it is the right time to go back to work. It's OK to be immersed in the baby stuff for a while. It's hard and unrelenting and when you go back too soon because you feel guilty or whatever, everyone suffers, including you.

- I like that I teach my kids about a working life and the associated responsibilities. They know if they want cool stuff like holidays, the money tree doesn't magically deliver. I also like that I teach them that women do many different jobs and being a mum is just one part of a bigger picture.

HUMAN BEING OR HUMAN DOING?

To develop a mindset that will sustain you through the peaks and troughs in life, you need to examine your beliefs about what is important. In modern life, we place value on action. People have become addicted to imaginary lists of things that need to get done. Your value should not come from what you do, but who you are. Are you a human being or a human doing? If your sense of achievement comes from getting to the end of a list each day or week, have you stopped to think about exactly what is on that list and if it really matters?

Most of us have internalised the importance of doing and have forgotten about the being. Get a visual of a plane in the sky. On one wing, there is the word 'being' and on the other, 'doing'. The plane is steady and balanced. But when we take one word off, the plane becomes tilted, and is at risk of crashing. How are you flying?

THE SINGLE BIGGEST FACTOR IN TAKING CHARGE OF YOUR EMOTIONAL FITNESS

The comforting feeling of being in control and enjoying overall happiness comes from our ability to fit everything we need, want and have to do into our lives. When we struggle to have everything in sync, we experience stress.

Not all stress is bad, though; we can use a certain amount of positive stress to make sure we are switched on when we need to be. But too much stress causes our bodies to produce an excess amount of the hormone cortisol. Once we have too much cortisol running through our systems, the wear and tear on our bodies can be major. Stress can interfere with our immune function and bone density and, in the long term, can play a role in things such as weight gain, high blood pressure, high cholesterol, heart disease … you get the picture. There isn't an area in your body that doesn't feel the effects of stress.

The single most important factor in decreasing stress and excess cortisol production is having a sense of control over all parts of our lives. If we feel like we are able to shape our lives, stress doesn't stand a chance of affecting us.

HEALTH — mind and body

WORK — career and achievements

RELATIONSHIPS — family, friends and colleagues

SOUL FOOD — whatever that means for you (spirituality, religion, your purpose and meaning, learning new things, fun and play)

The secret:
keep going.

SIX EMOTIONAL FITNESS STRATEGIES TO GET YOUR GAME ON

1. GIVE YOURSELF PERMISSION TO TAKE TIME OUT

Your brain is your most valuable tool, but it needs rest to achieve great output. Often when people are under the pump, they just work harder. But it's difficult to produce good work when you're exhausted. Surviving is not the same as thriving, and giving yourself permission to switch off is essential for your creativity.

You are likely to meet fierce opposition to this high-performance strategy. This is because our culture wrongly assumes that time out = laziness. However, research is now proving that while we are resting or simply having some mental downtime, our brains are still hard at work, replenishing the things that allow us to perform at our peak: attention, motivation, creativity and the energy required to be productive[2].

Rethinking your approach to downtime so it becomes an essential part of your routine is critical to success. Reframe your attitude from seeing breaks as a guilty pleasure to an important strategy for success. The kicker? If you want to do more, do less.

2. GET ENOUGH SLEEP

To declare you can survive on only a few hours of sleep has become something to beat your chest about. We brag about our sleep debt, but it is killing us and our creativity. In fact, bragging about your lack of sleep is equivalent to bragging about being drunk – you are cognitively impaired.

If you are serious about getting your game on, getting more sleep is the one thing that could make a dramatic difference. There is tons of clear evidence on how sleep, or lack thereof, affects your success[3]. It is a simple way of recharging and keeping our brains functioning at optimal level. But you have to make room for it in your life.

Take a lesson from the sporting arena. For athletes, sleep is on the same priority level as nutrition, training and all the other preparation they need to do to compete. They place such importance on sleep to help their performance that before game day some athletes spend a night or two away from their families to make sure they get the quality of sleep they need.

If you are looking for the best performance enhancer going (with the added benefits of being safe and legal), you have found it in sleep.

What level of priority do you give sleep? How are your sleeping habits affecting your ability to be the best you can be?

3. FUEL YOUR BODY

Do you think of food as a fuel source for your most important asset – your mind – or do you see it differently? If you are continually putting the wrong food in your body, you are not getting the best out of yourself, physically *and* mentally. The brain needs the good stuff to ensure great performance, just like our other muscles.

We get particularly scared when we see leaders eating badly. If you are managing others, there is even more reason to promote food as fuel for great performance. It might be easier to eat fast or pre-packaged food, or reach for the 3 pm choccie bar, but once you make the connection between food as fuel and an improvement in your performance, it's hard to keep eating the same way.

What are you feeding your mind? What rubbish are you telling yourself to make your food habits and choices seem OK?

4. EXERCISE

We are sure you are smart enough to have worked out the benefits of exercise already, so we will get straight to the point. Exercise is a great stress-buster and it's amazing the kind of creative thinking that can happen on a run or during a spin class – the idea for this book, for example. It not only has short- and long-term benefits physically, but mentally too (even being shown to assist with depression[4]). Too often though, exercise is put at the bottom of the to-do list or in the too-hard basket. We get the reasons, but we prefer to call the reasons excuses. One thing that often helps bump exercise up the list is to link it to reaching your overall potential. Exercise is a tool that can help you to achieve your goals and maintain or even improve your health.

5. BREATHE

Most people will not even notice how shallow their breath is, particularly when under stress. Breathing is automatic but, like everything else, the way we do it is habitual. Deep breathing (or conscious breathing) can reduce stress by helping you to control your nervous system and encourage your body to relax, bringing about increased feelings of calm and wellbeing. You can do it anywhere, at anytime. You don't need a candlelit room and rainforest music (but if that is your thing, go for it!).

6. FIT IN FUN AND PLAY

Before we grow up, fun and play are an integral part of our lives, but as the chaos of adulthood sets in, we tend not to make time for pure fun. Most adult activities are structured and function as goal-kicking opportunities; a sense of guilt has developed around building fun into our schedules. But losing yourself in a moment of fun and play can be totally refreshing, and it can fire up your creativity, imagination and problem-solving abilities, too. It can also improve your connection to others and boost your energy. It's an all-round emotional fitness enhancer.

In all the elite sporting environments we have been in, fun and play are serious success strategies. To relieve the pressure of performing to win, teams will play games (that are not their sport) and take part in fun, sometimes silly, activities that bring people together and give them a chance to unwind. When was the last time you did something purely for fun? What kinds of things do you like to do just for the sake of it? What did you love to do for fun in your childhood that you could incorporate back into your life as a grown-up?

Start somewhere.

Other ideas to energise you and ignite your brain muscle:

- Add a mental workout to your schedule. Challenge your intellect and memory by learning a new language or doing a Sudoku or crossword.

- Try something new. Have a conversation with someone new about something you've never discussed before.

- Learn a new skill. Learning strengthens your 'grey matter' by developing new neural pathways. Try playing a sport, mastering a craft or cooking a cuisine that is new to you.

- Keep your blood pressure low by making smart lifestyle choices. High blood pressure (hypertension) damages the blood vessels and increases the risk of stroke, which can contribute to mental decline.

- Use your non-dominant hand while performing a daily task (while brushing your teeth, for example). By using the opposite hand, you boost activity in a different hemisphere of the brain, giving you a chance to flex your mental muscle.

EMOTIONAL FITNESS CHALLENGES

If you have any emotional fitness challenges that you know are holding you back, have the courage to make working through them a priority. Get a support team around you (friends, family, professionals) to help you sort through the challenges. Let go of the fear of asking for help and do what is going to help you achieve your ambitions. Emotional fitness is an ongoing project with different areas requiring your focus from time to time. Don't let these challenges hold your best self back, and don't just think about the big challenges; try working through a couple of small things that will give you an edge.

Leigh's Story

I have always been someone who thrives on many things happening at once. I love to have a lot on my plate and, coupled with perfectionist behaviour, sometimes my emotional fitness can come under threat. I aspire to be an achiever in all areas of my life, including having a dynamic and impactful career and being a great mum and partner. (Of course, not necessarily in that order.) My mind can go into overdrive, and I can forget that recharging is important to create the sustained energy I need to stay at the top of my game.

I have learned the hard way over time about what happens when I don't look after myself, and the impact that too much cortisol surging through my body can have. I am not bullet proof, no matter how much I like to think I am.

My body gives me signs when I'm pushing it too much, and when I ignore them, it starts screaming at me through migraines and hormonal challenges that totally interfere with my sense of life control and happiness. In the past, I have been stuck in bed for three days at a time with migraine attacks, and for some days after I wouldn't feel my best and would miss out on the things I had worked so hard to be a part of.

Lying on my acupuncturist's bench once, after once again going to her complaining of being exhausted, I was asked two simple questions that highlighted the need to do things differently. She simply asked me, what did I do for time out and when did I give my body and mind a chance to recover?

The answers, somewhat shamefully, had become 'nothing and never'. I couldn't label one time in my week when I recharged. And worse than that, when asked what I liked doing in my downtime for fun, I found it difficult to pick something. Instead, I found I had been using any quiet time I had to think of the next thing to do, get more done or tick something off the list. I realised it wasn't sustainable and I would be back in her office (and other medical practitioners' offices) at regular intervals if nothing changed.

It's an ongoing challenge for me to do the things that I know 'fill my cup' – exercise, reading, socialising, cooking, getting to the beach (where I feel great) good sleep and productive downtime – which means that I really have to avoid the temptation of using downtime to get things done. I don't always find it easy to prioritise these things, but it is worth doing. I'm happier, calmer, more creative and clearer about what's important for me to achieve.

COPING WITH LIFE'S HECTIC PACE

We live in a world where we are constantly wired; we're tuned in 24/7 to what is happening, through all sorts of technology and platforms. Of course, it isn't always a bad thing to be so connected and up-to-date; making the most of opportunities the internet and social media provides is great. What is not so great is constantly feeling like our brains are switched on and processing information.

Mindfulness is one of the best coping strategies for this feeling, and it has become increasingly popular over the past few years for good reason. Simply put, mindfulness is the ability to be genuinely present in the moment, giving you relief from overthinking and racing around like a chook with its head cut off.

You know how we like to keep it real, right? We must admit, we used to think mindfulness wasn't for us and that it was really just for hippies who seem to have

all the time in the world to just sit, chill, think and do yoga. It just seemed too easy. Sit and do nothing, and that helps you be your best self? In the end, the benefits of mindfulness became clearer and we couldn't argue with it, so we jumped in and gave it a try. And guess what? We found the so-called hippies were onto something.

Mindfulness has surged in the treatment of stress, anxiety, depression and other physical and mental illnesses. There is much scientific evidence for the incredible effects that mindfulness has on our brains[5]. And now just about everyone is realising its benefits for stress relief and improving focus and performance. It gives us a break from being constantly connected to our phones and computers, and allows us to be still and understand our thoughts – to completely switch off.

Simply think of mindfulness as brain hygiene. In the same way you brush your teeth, you want to give your mind a chance to freshen up. You need to make sure that, aside from sleep, your brain has a chance to stop.

Mindfulness and meditation don't have to be complicated. There are so many free resources and apps out there that allow you to learn and practise in your own time, no matter how busy you are. Don't dress your excuses up as reasons. Try a few of these resources and see the difference they make to you.

Like everything, you get better when you practise, so don't expect to become a mountain-sitting yogi overnight. Your mind may wander quickly and often when you first try it out. The trick is to not be judgemental of your thoughts; just be conscious of where your mind goes, and then gently bring your focus back to the exercise.

Bianca's Story

I'm fairly new to the trend of meditation and mindfulness, having only discovered it in the past few years. When I was an athlete, I was always so focused on my body and just learned to tough things out. To me, life was seemingly about working as hard as I could until I couldn't do it anymore. I subscribed to that philosophy for far too long. I lived a life (and sometimes still do) of busy chaos. I enjoy being busy; I like to get a lot done and prefer it when every day is different. I spend hours on my phone or whatever Apple device I have on me at the time … I love my technology! But this isn't always healthy; sometimes I need to just STOP.

So why don't we all take better care of our brains when they're not working or feeling their best? I didn't have a light-bulb moment that made me believe in the power of mindfulness, but I did start to understand that meditation isn't just for new-agers that chant to the universe. I started to notice more conversation about it on social media and, as a bit of an experiment, I downloaded the Smiling Mind app and listened to it at night before I fell asleep.

The more I listened, the better awareness I had of my own body. I then found I slept better, even when my body was very tired and sore from training.

Mindfulness is about being present, making sure I take time out to be still, with no chaos and no phone. It ensures I just STOP and give my brain some rest and reconnect with my body. If you haven't tried it, you need to. Trust me.

Switch on to switch off

We all have our smartphones on us all the time, so why not use them to help us switch off?

Here are some apps you can use to help you explore the world of mindfulness and meditation:

- Smiling Mind
- 1 Giant Mind
- ReachOut Breathe
- The Mindfulness App
- Omvana – Meditation for Everyone

MOTIVATION

Have you found the secret elixir that gives you infinite amounts of motivation? If only it were that easy.

This isn't the time for us to embrace each other's excuses as to why we can't seem to find the motivation to do something; it's time to forget what we have or haven't done, pull our socks up and get it together! No more excuses. No more time wasting.

It's time for us all (and yes, we're included) to find the self-control, will power and resilience to make things happen in our lives.

We could give you the definition of motivation, but that's probably not going to be that helpful. What eludes most of us is what to do when we can't find any motivation, or when we have absolutely no desire to do something we know we should.

Going to the gym, eating healthily, starting a business, cleaning the house, or simply just getting out of bed in the morning and getting your day started can be extremely hard at times. Rest assured, you're not alone.

If you have a passion or dream that you can't stop thinking about then it is time to stop procrastinating and start figuring out what will work for you while you're searching for some of that secret elixir.

Are you in or are you out?

What drives your behaviour? There are two types of motivation. The first is the fuel you find within yourself: intrinsic motivation, which helps you achieve goals associated with personal satisfaction or enjoyment. Getting something in return is not the primary focus; you do it because you genuinely want to and it is important to you.

Extrinsic motivation fires you up in a different way; it is more about being motivated to act because something might come to you in return (for example, working hard on a project to get a promotion or entering a competition to win a prize), or to avoid punishment (for example, working hard at uni to avoid failing a subject).

Extrinsic motivation comes from stuff around you; intrinsic comes from within. Both can drive you, but intrinsic motivation has been shown to have a longer lasting impact on your activity levels. If you are doing something for the love of it, or the fun of it, rather than for external rewards (such as money or possessions), chances are you will be sustained for much longer.

So, what really motivates you? Are you tuned in to your internal motivators and do you use them as a source of energy for what you want and need to get done? Or are you waiting for something outside of yourself to tap you on the shoulder and give you a good enough reason to get going?

Motivating Team You

Do you have some structure in your life? We often go searching for motivation when we don't have a set routine or schedule to keep us on track. Most things in life are underpinned by repetition, routine and having a diary that is fairly well organised. It might be time consuming to have to schedule what's happening with Team You, but it saves a lot of time that you can then spend working towards that end point you've been thinking about. If you have a goal, you need to make it happen by having a plan, not by relying solely on motivation to get you there. Here are some strategies that have worked for us and might work for you:

Who do you love being around? Who are the people that add to your vibe and make you feel like you are invincible? Go and hang out with them, or give them a call.

Have you ever set a goal in your life? What is it? Write it down. Writing things down and telling others about it makes us far more accountable and almost guilts us into following through.

Stop complaining; it helps nobody and is really annoying to be around. Start picking yourself up every time you throw out excuses like, 'I'm too busy', 'I'm too tired', etc. It might be the case, but saying it out loud makes you believe — and then act like — it is reality. It doesn't have to be!

be your best self

List your current emotional fitness strategies. What works best for you? What do you need to try, start or stop doing to ensure you are high on your own priority list?

Pick a goal and write down the 'what, why and how'. What is it exactly that you want to do? Once you have that clear, have the end goal in mind when you answer the why and how. Why do you want to do it and what are the motivating (intrinsic and extrinsic) factors behind your goal? How will you know when you have achieved it?

Do it now.
Sometimes 'later' becomes 'never'

WINNING PLAYS

- USING THE BODY *AND* MIND IS CRUCIAL IN NAILING THE CAREER AND LIFE YOU ASPIRE TO.

- YOU NEED TO FIND A BALANCE BETWEEN HUMAN BEING AND HUMAN DOING TO BE SUCCESSFUL.

- MINDFULNESS IS NOT SOFT, IT'S A SMART STRATEGY.

- DON'T WAIT TO BE MOTIVATED TO DO ANYTHING. THE MOTIVATION WILL LIKELY COME AFTERWARDS, NOT BEFORE.

- DAILY RITUALS HELP REFOCUS THE LEVEL OF MOTIVATION YOU REALLY NEED.

mind games

The potential derailers the competition don't want you to work on

What sort of games are you playing with yourself? What kinds of things are on repeat in your head? These are the ideas that go around and around until you are convinced that they are real. Mind games are genuine showstoppers. They are self-sabotaging and we want you to cut them out right now. It's time to get tough with yourself in a different way and work out where the real enemy lies … it might be in your own head.

The good news? You have the power to change it. You are in control of this stuff. So let's get it sorted and get you on your way.

> You have brains in your head. You have feet in your shoes. You can steer yourself any direction you choose. You're on your own. And you know what you know. And YOU are the guy who'll decide where to go.
>
> – DR. SEUSS

CHAPTER 4
FEAR

> To fear is one thing.
> To let fear grab you by
> the tail and swing you
> around is another.
>
> – KATHERINE PATERSON

If we could have just one superpower, it would be the ability to dial down the fear response in people, so that life could be easier and all the worry, pain and misery caused by being stuck in fear could be avoided. Of course, we all fear different things, but the *effect of fear* is the same: we get stuck in a holding pattern and, consequently, this moves us even further away from what we are truly capable of.

What is your poison of choice when it comes to fear? Fear of failure? Fear of being wrong? Fear of what people will think? Fear of the unknown?

Imagine for a second the kind of place our world would be and what we would achieve, if we were able to be free of the fear that threatens to derail us. What would you do if there were no nagging voice, no doubt in your mind and no energy drainers telling you it couldn't happen?

Without doubt, the number one thing we work on with people is fear, and we see first-hand the impact these doubts and anxieties can have on life. They can hold you back from saying what you need to, doing what you are passionate about and having a real impact on the world (both yours and those around you).

WHAT YOU NEED TO KNOW ABOUT FEAR

▲ Fear is a normal function of our brains. It's often our first response to new information.

▲ In some situations fear is totally helpful (for example, when a threat presents itself, your brain and body work together to keep you alert), but in most situations in modern life, there is no need for our fear response to activate.

▲ The fear response is a strong force and it takes work to move through it. You have the power to shift fear to another, more productive emotion.

▲ Nobody escapes feeling fear. Not even those people who say they are fearless. Our culture places great emphasis on heroes and celebrating heroic acts that are about being brave and overcoming fear. Don't let this make you feel alone with your fears. We are all more similar than we'd care to admit. When people say they don't feel fear, it usually means they have worked on a few strategies to keep it from holding them back.

Fear is sometimes hard to identify because it disguises itself so well as rational thinking. What if I fail? What if I'm thinking too big? What will people think? If there is any sense of perceived risk, you will rationalise reasons not to do it and talk yourself out of it. And unless you challenge yourself, this might appear like sensible and appropriate thinking. Ask yourself these two questions:

1. WHAT IS THE EVIDENCE BASE FOR THIS LINE OF THINKING?

Most times, you will not be able to come up with hard evidence that backs up your fearful thoughts. In fact, what you will often find is that there is evidence *all around* to the contrary. But you have to look for it. You have to force yourself to see the whole picture of what you are grappling with, rather than just the stuff you want to see.

Say you want to start a new business or apply for a new role or promotion, but are plagued by the what-ifs. What if it fails? What if I am bad at it? Instead of dwelling on those negative questions, focus on turning your thought process around. Where is the evidence that you will fail? How many times have you failed before? What will you do to ensure you are not bad at it? Who might you enlist to help you succeed? What is your game plan?

Ask enough questions and, chances are, you will find that there is very little evidence to support your thinking, as long as you are being honest with yourself.

2. WHAT IS THE WORST THAT CAN HAPPEN?

This is the very best coaching question we have come across, because it shifts panicked thinking almost immediately to allow real rational thinking to kick in (and not the pretend stuff we just talked about). Seriously, what is the worst that can happen – and can you live with it? Often, we build these skyscrapers in our minds about what could happen when, really, the evidence is stacked against it.

One of my goals in life was to become a CEO of a sporting organisation. I felt, and still do feel, I had a lot to give and had worked hard to be a genuine, heart-based leader. I have always been crazy about the challenges of leadership and working with athletes and staff to be the best they can be.

I had been working towards getting the experience I needed, in a variety of roles, when the role of Netball Victoria CEO came up. The position description intrigued me. The opportunity intrigued me. I wanted to apply, but the voice inside my head came up with lots of reasons not to: my age (I was 33 at the time), my lack of experience, a couple of kids, fear of what people would think, blah, blah, blah. I can make up excuses dressed as reasons for hours on end.

But I really wanted to give it a crack and couldn't stop thinking about it. So I started testing the water a bit. First, I told my then boss about my aspiration. He didn't fall over with laughter, surprisingly. Then, my mentors insisted I should apply. I didn't tell my partner, because I was afraid of what he might think. I called the recruiter. He told me that I was an outside chance, if I'm lucky, but to put my application in nonetheless.

'An outside chance.' I could take this comment in one of two ways. I could give up right there or I could decide that 'an outside chance' was better than no chance

Leigh's Story

at all. Besides, he hadn't given me an outright 'no'. I appreciated his honesty and something stirred in me, so I stopped focusing on the outcome and concentrated on what the experience of going through the process might bring.

Out of many applicants, I was shortlisted. Suddenly, it felt very real! What if I didn't get it? What if I DID get it? I focused on staying rational – there was no evidence to suggest I couldn't do it. I had the capacity to keep learning, put good people around me and make a plan. One step at a time! I decided that rather than worrying about the odds, I was going to embrace them. I had a one-in-four chance – I would take it. I focused on that and my performance, rather than what the others that had been shortlisted might be doing. I prepared for the interview by thinking about what I could do to stand out. I didn't know everything and they knew it, so I wasn't going to pretend. Instead, I was going to show the panel what I DID know and the sort of person I was. I walked out of the interview like I had just run a marathon – I was stuffed. I couldn't have given it any more and had learned so much about myself in the process. I was proud.

By the way, I got the job, which was something of a surprise to my partner, not because he didn't believe I could do it but because I was so worried about his thoughts on applying, I had kept it from him. He was so thrilled for me. Lesson learned – don't waste energy on making assumptions about what people might think. There is always an outside chance you are wrong. Take it.

STRESS AND FEAR ARE EXCELLENT MATES

When Stress and Fear get together, they can have one hell of a good time. When we are stressed, our fear response can overreact, sending us into a spin, which can lead to snap decisions. In these moments we can become paralysed, or act in ways that are not in our best interests. Stress and Fear then invite their mate Regret along and bingo – a perfect party begins.

This is definitely not the kind of party you want to go to. So, to avoid attendance, the first thing to do is recognise when stress and fear may cause you to make poor decisions. When is your stress response triggered? Does it come from a base of fear? Be specific about exactly what you are stressed about, or afraid of, and determine what you need to do to reduce the stress and fear. Being able to identify your feelings and let them go takes practice. But learning to get out of your own way is one of the most important things you can do to ensure your success.

WHAT'S DRIVING YOUR FEAR? GET CLEAR ABOUT IT

Usually, there are patterns or habits surrounding everyone's fears. Getting clear on what triggers and drives your fears is helpful. Step back, lady, and reassess your fears through a new lens. Is there a pattern or consistent theme you notice? What are the situations that bring fear out in you? Thinking about these ahead of time helps you to manage them better when you are in the moment. And a tip: don't get too 'Judge Judy' here. You want to remain curious about your patterns of behaviour, and how they help or hinder you. The goal is to remain observant; develop your 'feardar' (your fear radar, get it?) to understand what scares you the most. This will help you prepare for situations before they happen.

WHAT SCARES YOU THE MOST? GOOD, NOW GO TOWARDS IT

Our natural instinct is often to move well away from what makes us fearful. But one way to deal with your fear is to experience it, examine it and work out that the thing that induces it is not nearly as scary as you thought. Of course, there are limitations to this strategy. Don't go and do dumb life-threatening stuff, for example. But do go and test your fears out a bit. If your fear is public speaking, the only way to move past it is to move through it. This might mean breaking the fear down into bite-size chunks, slowly prodding the comfort zone.

20 SECONDS OF COURAGE

One of the best techniques we have learned to deal with our fears and be courageous is the '20 seconds of courage' strategy that you can easily apply to your fears. Undertaking big courageous acts can be overwhelming, so next time you need to dig deep, try it for just 20 seconds. Often, this is all the time required to get over the initial inner hurdle of making a start – say yes, say no, approach someone you have wanted to talk to, give the feedback you need to, or jump out of that plane. We can all fake courage for 20 seconds, and what you might find after the initial 20 seconds is up, is that you are able to tap into reserves of courage you didn't even know you had.

Be your best self

Fear is the enemy of success. What do you fear? When does it come up for you? For the next few days (or whatever timeframe you need), try to prioritise courage over security. Identify your irrational thoughts and work out what is the worst that could happen. *Visualise* yourself dealing with the fear and moving through it. Pick a small action that will move you *towards* this place. You only need 20 seconds of courage to change something – what will be your 20-second task today?

Go the extra mile. It's never Crowded.

WINNING PLAYS

- NOBODY ESCAPES FEELING FEAR. YOUR JOB IS NOT TO TRY AND ERADICATE IT, BUT TO PRACTISE MOVING THROUGH IT.

- WHAT IS THE WORST THAT CAN HAPPEN? ASKING THIS QUESTION KEEPS YOU COURAGEOUS.

- 20 SECONDS OF COURAGE IS ALL YOU NEED TO GET STARTED.

CHAPTER 5
INNER CRITICS AND TYRE-KICKERS

Inner critic The voice in one's head that produces a pattern of thoughts, usually negative, sometimes destructive, never helpful

Tyre-kicker Someone not really truly interested in you, who is quick to point out all the negatives, or reasons things can't happen

When we are striving towards our goals, it is important that we are well supported. To be successful, you need to have the right mindset and a great team around you. Each elite sporting team we have worked with has focused on getting these two elements right while shutting out the white noise as much as possible.

White noise comes from two places: *internally* (the 'inner critic') and *externally* (other people and what they think).

The one thing that you can control on the road to success is the amount of interference you have from these internal and external sources.

We acknowledge you can't control people or other environmental factors, but you *can* control how you respond and how much you take on their beliefs and attitudes.

Your job is to strip away as much interference as possible to give yourself the best possible chance of succeeding. If you don't, it is easy to get off track. Interference is like really bad background music or a loud hum in your ears. Calling it white noise also works because it indicates just how loud and frustrating it can be.

What kinds of things do you say to yourself to keep things safe and comfy? They might include:

I'm not good enough.

I don't have the experience.

I will never be able to do that.

THE INNER CRITIC

Most of us wouldn't talk to our worst enemy the way we talk to ourselves – but often we don't think of it this way, and we certainly don't see the incredibly negative impact this kind of self-talk has on our self-esteem, confidence and performance.

Our inner critic lives most of the time in our unconscious processes – neatly tucked away where no one can see, right?

Wrong. The irony of the inner critic is that it is most visible in our behaviours, our relationships with others and the relationship we have with ourselves (which of course affects our behaviours, which impacts our relationships with others ... a nice, neat, complete circle of unhelpful stuff).

One of the goals of the inner critic is to keep us safe and comfortable. So the inner critic can be useful in some ways – it keeps us alert to potential dangers. The thing is though, the inner critic is often too loud; it becomes an all-consuming voice that doesn't serve to help us when the volume is turned up too high. So, what is the volume like at the party inside your head?

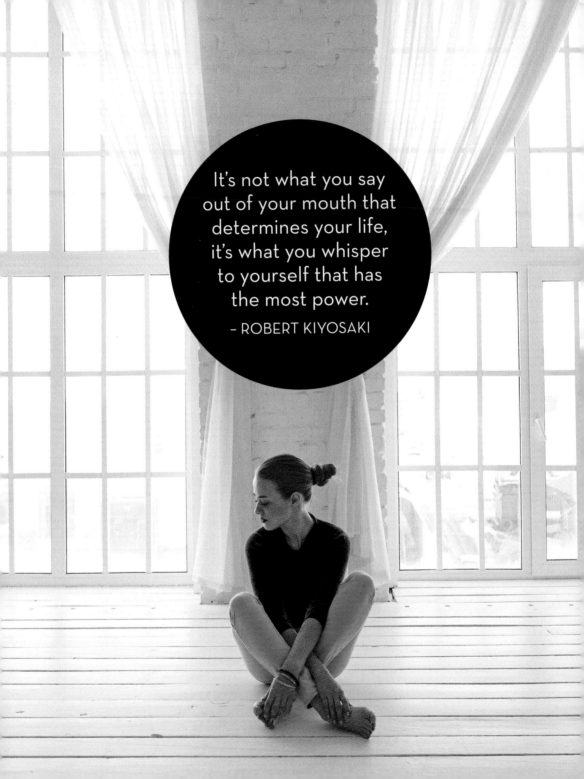

It's not what you say out of your mouth that determines your life, it's what you whisper to yourself that has the most power.

– ROBERT KIYOSAKI

Trying to live a perfect life

One of the major pursuits of the inner critic is the pursuit of perfection. The quest for perfection can go deep, and the pressure you put on yourself can be unrelenting (and totally unhelpful).

Trying to be perfect all the time not only changes your behaviour, but it is downright exhausting. It takes a lot of energy to be perfect, or make something perfect. All the judgements you place on yourself, the stress, the tension and that constant feeling of being on edge take their toll. While having high standards is a good thing, setting them so high that you constantly fail robs you of experiencing a sense of achievement and happiness. **The problem with perfectionism is that it doesn't ever give you the chance to feel good about yourself.** If this is a theme for you (and you are not alone here), then your wellbeing is at risk in so many ways. Increased stress, frustration, anger, worry, as well as lack of sleep, to name a few, can lead to significant challenges for you on a personal and professional front.

Perfection is a façade

Here's the thing: there is no such thing as perfect. While it is well intentioned, perfection is a totally made-up idea, and completely subjective. However, lots of us base our judgements about ourselves on the unrealistic mental model of perfection and always fall short. In fact, the standards we set may not even reflect what is realistic or achievable, but we try to get there anyway. You can get hooked on feeling awesome only when things are perfect, which means you feel bad about yourself when things are not, which leads to more disappointment – you get the idea. For us, this is the definition of insanity.

Just stop here and really think about perfection as a façade for a moment – we place a huge amount of emphasis on something that actually doesn't exist, and allow ourselves to

> Perfectionism is the murderer of all good things.
> – ELIZABETH GILBERT

be controlled by it. How? Perfectionism is never ending because, in our eyes, we haven't met the standards yet. And after a so-called failure, perfectionists will either give up altogether, or work harder. The cycle starts again …

Moving the goal posts

If they ever actually meet their very high expectations, perfectionists (just to put the icing on their perfect cake) like to reset the bar even higher next time. In other words, they move the goal posts because they see their success as a fluke. Re-read this paragraph … we are exhausted just writing it.

The paradox of perfectionism

Most people who want to be perfect are actually defeating the purpose of their efforts. Having high standards and working tirelessly to maintain them can hinder performance rather than enhance it. It's a strange paradox to get your head around, but really it's about the notion that working harder is not always working smarter. Working harder could just be … well, working harder.

There is a crack in everything, that's how the light gets in.

– LEONARD COHEN

Leigh's story

I would absolutely say that I have a tendency towards perfectionism, and have done for as long as I remember. I can't really recall a time in the early years where I wasn't working hard, striving for success and sometimes tying myself up in knots trying to get there. But for a long time, I also felt like a fraud. If I achieved something, my inner critic would scream loudly at me, *fluke*! Each role in leadership I landed, I was waiting for someone to tap me on the shoulder and tell me that actually, they were joking when they gave me the job. I was, in some ways, waiting to be found out, which drove me to work tirelessly to make sure I was one step ahead. I would make sure I did it all and didn't rely on anyone.

The problem was, that by doing it all, I wasn't giving anyone a chance to either help or bring their strengths to the table. In reality, I really wasn't being an effective team player. I got a piece of feedback once that led me to change my ways. At a review of my performance, I was told that I was indeed good at my job, but needed to learn to 'take other people on the journey' – meaning I forgot to take other people with me … a huge flaw for a leader! I needed to learn to delegate, seek others' views and sell the vision. These were all issues of control, as I wanted things to be perfect. But in striving for perfection, I actually missed the mark entirely.

Some perfectionist behaviours

While the following behaviours can impact your stress levels and mood in negative ways, importantly, they also impact your relationships, having implications for how you lead and the kind of success you can have throughout your career.

You procrastinate
You put things off for fear that they will not be done well enough, and find it hard to make decisions for fear of deciding the wrong thing.

You don't know when to change tack
You can't acknowledge when a strategy is in decline because you have invested too much in getting it 'right'.

You take too much time
You are deliberately slow so you don't miss anything.

You avoid things
You don't take any risks for fear of it not working out, or being told 'no'.

You can't (won't) delegate
You fear other people won't do as good a job as you.

You are obsessed with excessive lists/organising
You create lists on lists!

You quit
You stop before anyone finds out you made a mistake.

Instead of perfection, strive for excellence

Excellence and perfection are two different things. Both allow you to set high standards and challenge yourself to get there, but one won't get in the way of your sense of self-worth. Striving for personal excellence is about being your best, and not about being better than before.

What would really happen if ... ?

To change your mindset, think about these questions: what would really happen if I … took a bit of time off? Didn't clean up after dinner? Handed in a report that was good, but not perfect? There are things in life that require, in fact, demand perfection (such as airline safety and emergency department procedures) but really, outside of potential life and death situations, *what would really happen?* What is the cost to you to spend excessive amounts of time making something perfect when good will do?

THE TYRE-KICKERS

Just as the inner critic can be too loud, so can the outer critics. You know the ones – the energy drainers, the ones in your life that tell you all the time how it can't happen, rather than lifting you up and supporting you.

We hear consistently from all sources – be it successful business people, athletes, or our mentors – that those you surround yourself with are critical to success. One popular saying we think is spot on is, 'you become like the five people you spend most of your time with'.

If these five people are nay-sayers, there will be no happy ending. We need to be frank here. You need to get rid of these types if you are serious about achieving your goals.

It sounds blunt, and we know it won't be easy, but the people that suck your energy, or serve as your 'outer critics', are not genuinely in your corner and serve no positive purpose.

Wabi-sabi your mindset

Applying the Japanese principle of wabi-sabi can help you deal with things as they are, not as you imagine them to be. It's a mindset – and a way of living – that finds beauty in imperfection and accepting the natural cycles or rhythms of life, from birth to death. Authenticity is king. There are three things that wabi-sabi powerfully reminds us: that nothing lasts, nothing is finished and nothing is perfect. These are things perhaps we know intuitively, but the modern, shiny version of self we put out for everyone to see is at odds with this.

We wabi-sabi our mindsets to bring us back to what is truly important, to remind us that no matter what stage we are at, we are absolutely perfectly imperfect.

How to spot the tyre-kickers:

▲ They have a victim mindset, they blame everyone and everything else for their problems and never take responsibility.

▲ They complain and make excuses (over and over again).

▲ They thrive on drama and jump from one bad situation to the next, or make molehills into mountains.

And, most importantly, if you are still unsure, think about the people who make you feel exhausted — a sure sign that they are the drainers in your life.

be your best self

What is your white noise? What keeps you up at night? Is it internal or external? List some strategies that will help you turn the volume down so your true voice can be heard.

Think about the different areas of life — career, leadership, health, wellbeing, sport and relationships, as well as the day-to-day stuff like housework and organising your life. Where does perfectionism enter? What is the true cost (stress, worry, etc.)? Can you identify when the behaviour is at its peak and when it is in decline?

WINNING PLAYS

- THE INNER CRITIC, WHILE TUCKED AWAY INSIDE, IS VISIBLE IN EVERYTHING YOU DO.

- THERE ARE DIFFERENT WAYS TO BE A PERFECTIONIST, BUT THE RESULT IS ALWAYS THE SAME – YOUR RELATIONSHIPS AND YOUR CHANCES OF SUCCESS ARE NEGATIVELY IMPACTED.

- TYRE-KICKERS ARE EVERYWHERE. HOW MUCH SPACE YOU GIVE THEM IS UP TO YOU.

CHAPTER 6
UNHOOK YOURSELF

FAILURE

The truth about failure is that it is a totally necessary part of reaching our goals. The person who doesn't make mistakes is probably not making much at all. And yet, most of us are so scared of failing, that we spend an enormous amount of energy worrying about it, avoiding it and definitely not talking about it as part of the success tool kit. These days, only seeing #shinysuccess doesn't help – it gives us a false account of what true journeys to success look like. If we set failure up as the enemy, then we can't truly use the experience of failure to help us move forward.

Think about children learning a new skill like riding a bike (or even babies learning to walk). They fail many times before they master it, and we cheer them on through every failure, knowing they are heading towards achievement. But somehow, we lose this attitude towards failure when we become adults, and rather than see it as a step towards achieving our goals, we see it as a giant step away from them.
How do you view failure? What role has it played in your life?

Giving failure way too much airplay

Failure is given way too much credit. We build skyscrapers in our minds about what *might* happen, usually in a negative sense. We minimise the positives that might come from giving something a go because we set failure up as catastrophic and permanent. This line of thinking puts us into a holding pattern, rather than moving us forward. Failure may or may not be catastrophic, but it certainly doesn't have to be permanent.

Success flows when you throw yourself in and have a go – mistakes and all!

– EMMA ISAACS

The culture around failure feeds us messages like, 'failure is not an option', 'failure is for people who don't plan' and 'it is shameful to make a mistake'. These messages can be powerful behaviour modifiers. The beliefs we hold about failure determine how we deal with it, in relation to ourselves and others.

Failure as opportunity

Rather than see failure as some sort of death, we need to see it as an opportunity (a birth, if you like). Failure gives us all sorts of information that we can use to dust ourselves off and get going again. It's an opportunity to reset our focus, to use the additional information to sharpen our strategies or to stop flogging a dead horse. Seeing it purely as information – what didn't work and what we learned about ourselves – is critical success-journey data. By avoiding failing (or at least having a high fear of failure), we deny ourselves the very data – the grist for the mill – that will help us move towards our goals. The irony is that avoiding situations where you might fail or make mistakes stunts your growth and development, which over time may cause you to make more mistakes.

Put the pain behind you

Feelings of shame, embarrassment and isolation put anything that we may have learned from an experience in the background for our workplaces and ourselves.

It is painful to acknowledge when you don't achieve your goals, but by talking about it and having a positive mindset, you can learn from it. The only really 'bad' failure is the one that you can't, or won't, learn from. Attitude is paramount. If you think it is catastrophic and/or permanent, it will be. It's what you do *after* you fail that is the most important thing, not the failure itself.

HOOKED ON
THE OPINIONS OF OTHERS

From the minute we wake up in the morning, we are consumed by what people might think about the small things — from what people think of your jeans, for example — to bigger things, like what your colleagues think when you speak up. We wonder, we analyse, we make ourselves sick over them.

And that is just the people we know. We are also hooked on what people we *don't know* might think. It's exhausting!

Living that kind of life, constantly mentally checking what others may think, is a big mind game.

The impact of being hooked on others' opinions

Being hooked on what other people think (or, in other words, needing their approval) comes at a great cost to your performance. Approval-seeking, even if you are only doing this passively, can cause procrastination, worry, fear and self-doubt. All these emotions and the resulting inaction gets in the way of creativity and can make you withdraw, say what you don't really mean and withhold ideas. Even if you are able to sustain high levels of performance while being hooked on approval, chances are, you are burnt out — you don't have any time for yourself, don't say no when you should and you worry and work too hard.

When you work on accepting yourself and being happy with your decisions, you don't need to be so hooked on seeking approval and acceptance from others.

What people *really* think?

The truth is, people don't really think about you as much as you think about yourself. Most of the time, overthinking and analysing what others are thinking is a waste of energy. There will only be a handful of people who are really giving you any more than a fleeting thought, and unless they are in your inner sanctum (see below), who cares what they think? If you let go of the battle, you will have more energy to put into being the kind of person YOU are happy with.

The inner sanctum

Sorting out who is in your inner sanctum – those with opinions and advice that really matter to you – is one way to unhook from what everyone thinks. In reality, this group is really small and usually includes the people who know you for who you really are: family, friends and trusted advisors. These are the ones that pass your 'get on a plane' test. If you were some distance away from them and, for whatever reason, needed them urgently, would they get on the plane for you without hesitation? These people are the only ones you need to hook on to.

You can't please everyone - so why are you trying?

It is impossible to please everyone all the time and live up to the expectations of others, but many of our actions are focused on this. But here's the thing, people are always judging, no matter what. No matter how much energy you put into people-pleasing, someone will be judging you. What is the worst thing that could happen if someone didn't agree with you, or didn't like you? What would *really* happen? At worst it will be temporarily uncomfortable and, at best, nothing will happen. Not a thing. The sun is still going to come up tomorrow, and you are going to get on with your life.

The person that thinks most about you is ... you.

However, what's the flip side? What's the best that could happen? You are authentically YOU. People will respect you for that. By unhooking from people's approval, you are able to go for the goals that are important to YOU, not others. Game on!

You become what you think

If you spend considerable time working out what others want, and then accommodating all requests, chances are you have become a people-pleaser. The problem with this is that your behaviour, while trying to avoid judgement, actually invites it. It becomes a self-fulfilling prophecy and you will find yourself back where you started, or worse, on an exhausting people-pleasing merry-go-round. Tired, anyone?

How to not give two hoots about what people think:

▲ Know yourself. Understand your values, and what is important to you. Once you have this self-knowledge, caring about what others think of you becomes less important. If you don't know yourself well, then it will be tempting to get this definition from others.

▲ Practise saying no when you really want to say no. Run a couple of initial experiments on this. Say no just once, to see what will really happen. Our hunch is, nothing much.

▲ Find a way to prod the edges of comfort and say something you really want to. Practise at meetings, with friends, wherever you have something to say. For this, you will need your 20 seconds of courage to do rather than think. Find one small situation to begin with, and then build to incorporate saying what you think as much as possible.

▲ Evaluate your tasks based on how hooked they are to approval. What are the things you do that are right for you, and what things are based on approval? Work through the people-pleasing list of activities and slowly reduce them, with the goal of eliminating them entirely.

THE COMPARISON GAME

Comparing ourselves with others is a clear path to insanity. It's so common it might almost be considered normal if it wasn't so destructive. And we say destructive because we bet that the comparisons you draw are not favourable ones. We rarely look at others and decide that we are doing OK. More often than not, we believe we come up short. Comparing yourself to others is a habit that can be deeply ingrained and hard to even recognise in ourselves.

And it's really hard to stop. It's tempting to look at something on social media, sigh and think, *that will never be me. I don't shape up. I'm so far behind.*

Admire someone else's beauty without questioning your own.

Why comparisons are useless:

▲ We often compare our everyday with someone else's #shinysuccess. You don't truly know other people's stories and the snippets you're comparing yourself to are often conveniently dressed up.

▲ No matter how successful you become, there will always be someone who appears to be doing better than you.

▲ Comparisons put the spotlight on the wrong person. You can't control any other life than your own. It is pointless to waste energy worrying about other people, unless you are trying to learn from their whole journey, and not just their highlight reel.

▲ You just end up feeling negative emotions, like resentment, towards yourself and where you are at, and sometimes even resentment towards others (for example, *why do they have that and I don't?*).

How to stop comparing:

▲ Realise that you are comparing apples with oranges. No-one is on your journey, and you can't be on anyone else's, nor can you know the truth behind their highlight reel.

▲ Stop and smell your own roses. Too often we gloss over our own successes or the things we do really well. It's human (but not helpful) to focus on the gaps. **You are enough, and always have been.** Your journey is unique and you have a unique contribution to make.

▲ If you need to compare, change the focus of your comparison and turn it inwards. Compete with yourself, not others. Aim to be a better version of yourself each day rather than an imitation of someone else. Being the best version of you is really the only game that is worth playing. Top athletes train by trying to do better tomorrow, and the day after that, and the day after that …

▲ Stay curious, rather than feeling resentful or envious. Focus on the right things

You will never influence the world trying to be like it.

when you look at others. What inspiration can you take? What would you do differently? What lessons can be learned?

▲ Above all, what helps is to define *your own* version of success (see p. 132 for more). If you hook yourself to that, you are less likely to end up playing the comparison game.

be your best self

When you notice yourself making unhelpful comparisons, practise redirecting your thoughts. You don't need to eradicate comparisons altogether, just shift the focus back to yourself. Draw up a table and label one column 'short term' and one column 'long term'. Ask yourself the following questions to help you focus on your own success:

● Short term: What wins of your own can you celebrate? What are you doing more of or less of that has changed the game for you during the past 12 months? What are you currently working on that will keep moving things forward for you?

● Long term: What are you doing now that you couldn't (or didn't think you could) have done a few years ago? How have things improved for you?

WINNING PLAYS

- FAILURE IS A GREAT TEACHER AND WE BENEFIT THE MOST WHEN WE SEE IT AS AN OPPORTUNITY, NOT A CATASTROPHE.

- FAILURE IS NOT PERMANENT AND NOT A GOOD PREDICTOR OF FUTURE SUCCESS.

- A LOT OF US GET HOOKED ON WHAT PEOPLE THINK, BUT IT STOPS US FROM TRULY BEING OUR BEST SELVES. WORK OUT WHAT'S IMPORTANT TO YOU AND THE OPINIONS YOU VALUE, AND LEAVE IT AT THAT.

- WHEN YOU COMPARE YOURSELF TO OTHERS (IN REAL LIFE OR ON SOCIAL MEDIA), LOOK FOR THE SIMILARITIES, NOT THE DIFFERENCES.

Take the lead

Leaping ahead of the game

We are here to dispel a big myth: leadership is not hard. We have all been duped. People love to complicate it, but keeping it simple works every time. There are three things you need to remember:

1. LEADING YOURSELF IS IMPORTANT.

In fact, it's just as important as leading others. Be in charge of yourself before you attempt to lead other people.

2. GREAT LEADERSHIP SKILLS SHOULD ALWAYS BE ON DISPLAY.

Don't wait for a shiny new job title – demonstrate leadership at every stage of your career.

3. LEADERSHIP IS A WORK IN PROGRESS.

You don't know it all and never will, but you get better at leadership the more you integrate it into your life.

There are a million books that focus on the mechanics of leadership, so we want to share practical insights that you can apply today. We want you to see leadership differently so you can get ahead of the game and have the greatest possible impact. Isn't that what we are all here to do?

A leader is
a dealer in hope.
– NAPOLEON BONAPARTE

CHAPTER 7
LEADERSHIP

Leadership is a critical part of our professional *and* personal lives but we often glorify it, as if there is a formula or it is a skill that only a chosen few have. Women also have unique challenges when it comes to leadership – many more men than women hold professional leadership roles and this has fostered the prevalence of just one (masculine) leadership style. As a consequence, bias is alive and well in many workplaces. We won't bore or depress you with the many statistics on this (things are slowly changing – with the emphasis on slow), but we will say that women's experience of bias in the workplace and other walks of life has an effect on their notion of what leadership really means. Expensive leadership courses that are seen as must-dos and articles like 'The 10 traits you need to be a leader' only perpetuate the myth that leadership is hard or attainable only for the chosen few – usually men. Added to this, there is now so much information published on the topic of leadership that if you started reading it today, you wouldn't get through it all in your lifetime.

Leadership is a way of LIFE.

Because men dominate the leadership space, women can feel intimidated, can lack confidence and can be held back by feelings of inadequacy. They approach leadership as though there is a checklist to get through before they can put their name forward. Anytime we have asked a room of women to raise their hands if they consider themselves as leaders, very few hands go up. It's not easy to claim your leadership power and think of yourself as a leader because the path to being one is often unclear.

While the system needs dismantling and reworking on so many levels, we simultaneously need to rethink what we know and understand about leadership so we can fully take on opportunities to lead, and have an impact, when they arise.

You might not be the 'boss' at work, but you can definitely be the leader of your own life.

– NAOMI SIMSON

Leadership myths busted

- **You need a fancy title to be a true leader**
  Big titles fire up the ego for about 30 seconds, but the shine will soon wear off. You don't need anything formal to lead. In fact, you are going to need to demonstrate your leadership skills way before a big role comes along.

- **There is only one leadership style that is effective**
  Chances are, if you try and lead others with one style, you will fail. Understanding different styles and having the ability to be flexible is crucial. The command and control days are over and being comfortable in your own leadership style – warts and all – is what it's all about.

- **You need a certain amount of experience to be a leader**
  Quality is more important than quantity – how you learn from and use past experiences is far more important than the amount of experience you have had. You can be a very effective young leader, but you can't go into it thinking you know it all – ever – no matter what your age.

Leaders have all the answers

You don't need to know everything to be a great leader. But you need to know how to get the answers you are looking for.

Leaders should be in the spotlight

Leadership requires a certain level of humility. Leaders that are constantly in the spotlight are doing it for their ego, not their team. If the spotlight is not for you, you can still be a great leader. It takes all styles to be truly successful.

Leaders are born, not made

This is the biggest myth we have ever heard. Leadership, like any other skill, can be learned. There is a science and art to leadership. Learning the science can be as simple as reading a couple of books. Learning the art requires effort over time, a willingness to take some risks and the courage to keep learning about yourself and others.

LEADING YOURSELF

Before you try and foster high performance in your team, you need to know yourself first. People tend to think the biggest challenge of leadership is leading others, but the real challenge lies with you. Looking in the mirror is by far the hardest thing to do. Knowing your strengths, vulnerabilities, opportunities to develop and how they impact on your relationships and work is vital.

Leading yourself means getting comfy with seeking feedback and being clear about the behaviours that help and the ones that hold you back. Consider these questions:

1. WHY DO YOU WANT TO LEAD?

Understand your purpose and values. How does leadership fit into that? Values matter, because what you think is important will shape your behaviour. Many people get into trouble when they are leading and living in ways that are in conflict with their personal values. Clarifying why you want to lead helps you through the tough times of leadership and anchors you to a bigger purpose.

2. WHY SHOULD YOU LEAD?

This question is not asked often enough. What do you bring to the table? How might you inspire others? How do you let others know that they matter? How do you develop excitement for a project, game or task?

Ask yourself these questions every few months or so to make sure you are focusing on the right things.

BEING FIT TO LEAD

Many workplaces don't prioritise health as a tool for great leadership. They are full of artificial light and are often surrounded by fast food joints. We are required to sit in front of screens for long periods of time and work in high-octane, high-pressure environments where being 'busy' is glamourised. We make long commutes to and from the office, often arriving home to eat more fast food because we don't have time to cook. This then affects how we sleep.

Our physical and mental health is our number one asset, so consistent good habits are essential (an occasional cheeseburger or a few drinks with the girls isn't what we're talking about here). **Our habits define who we are and – more than that – define the type of leader we can be.** After all, being at our peak (whatever that is for you), both mentally and physically, gives us a fighting chance to have an impact on the world. And that is the essence of what real leadership is about.

Go back and have a look at our emotional fitness strategies in Chapter 3 (see pp. 44–47). Take some time to understand your wellness and how it impacts your leadership potential. It will be time well spent.

> It's really true – you need to sleep your way to the top. Literally.
> – BIANCA AND LEIGH

> 'Restore connection' is not just for devices, it is for people too. If we cannot disconnect, we cannot lead.
> – ARIANNA HUFFINGTON

LEADING OTHERS

Make leading others simple. Think about what you value in leaders and make sure you live those values, consistently and repetitively. Leading others is as enjoyable as it is hard work. To stay on top of the game, you have to do the little big things right.

We're here for a reason.
I believe a bit of the
reason is to throw little
torches out to lead
people through the dark.

– WHOOPI GOLDBERG

Things to consider:

▲ Have a reflective and open mindset. Focus on keeping your mind curious, devising solutions and being open to new possibilities.

▲ Be humble. There is a saying that is used in sport a lot: 'They are drinking their own bath water'. It means someone has been seduced by their own hype. Not only is it super unattractive, it is risky. Listen to your team as much as you do your own voice.

▲ Get in the trenches with your team. Demonstrate as often as you can that you are willing to do what they do. Decisions that are made from ivory towers generally don't get genuine cut through. Roll up your sleeves. This earns you the moral mandate to lead, not just the title.

▲ Allow someone to signal to you when things go off course. You need feedback more than ever as a leader, but people can be wary of providing it to the hierarchy because it is usually handled badly. As a result, you might be the last to hear it. And when that person does give you feedback, genuinely listen. Don't focus on defending your behaviour. It's more important to know how you are perceived than the 'reality' in your head.

▲ Watch for your own biases. We can sometimes play favourites with certain people or groups, perhaps because we understand or like them better. And it's fairly easy to fall into the trap of stereotyping. Again, this is where your signaller (see point above) is useful.

▲ Do what you say you are going to do. Protect your leadership by following through on the promises or statements you make. If you can't follow through, tell your people. It's OK to be vulnerable, to admit mistakes and say how you plan to improve things in the future. Admit you don't know when you don't know. People want to be led by a real person who thinks through the issues, not a perfect person who can't reflect on performance and adjust where needed.

▲ Know and understand the difference between management and leadership. Different situations require different approaches.

BAD LEADERSHIP IS EVERYWHERE

So we have said that leadership isn't that complicated and given you some simple strategies to help lead yourself and others. So then, why is bad leadership everywhere, despite the thousands of books, courses and seminars on it? Why can't people seem to get their leadership game on? We all have horror stories of bad bosses and how they have affected us. We see the consequences of bad leadership in our companies and our governments – it's on the news almost daily.

The answer is that leadership has become about leaders, rather than about their people. Self-interest is rife in the leadership game, and building trust with people is a low priority. Abuse of power is always central to bad leadership. It starts with how people are recruited (either for their skills or for others reasons) and continues because most organisations don't utilise proper mechanisms to deal with bad leadership.

There are two things that are important here. First, bad leadership gives you an opportunity to stand out. Do the little things consistently, develop your self-awareness and have a plan in place to keep on top of your performance. It WILL make all the difference.

Second, remember you don't have to put up with bad leadership. Vote with your feet. You spend more time at work with your colleagues and leaders than you do with your loved ones. Make it count! If your boss is genuinely a bully, a narcissist, a tyrant or just plain incompetent, and you feel you have tried all you can, look to leave as soon as possible. Don't focus on being stuck there – focus on an exit strategy.

Leading an organisation is tough and definitely not glamorous (but totally worth it – it's incredibly rewarding). You have to lead up (usually to a board), lead across and lead down, often juggling multiple agendas and priorities.

My goal has always been to be a 'heart-based' leader, which means leading through people and taking an authentic approach (but definitely not a soft one). Sometimes, it has meant having to do things that I find hard, like delivering feedback, moving people on or saying no. But spending time understanding what strengths I bring to the table and what I don't necessarily do so well has helped me. I was exposed to instant, critical feedback often when I worked in the AFL. At the time I didn't really like it so much, but when I got into other leadership roles, I worked out what a gift it had been. Knowing myself, warts and all, meant that nothing much surprised me. It also meant that I could focus on what I was good at.

When I moved to netball, the culture was a fair bit different to what I was used to.

Leigh's story

Leading a volunteer-based board with big personalities (but not necessarily business nous) was a huge challenge. Working with very limited resources after being in high-performance environments with big budgets was also a challenge. These challenges really tested the value of my heart-based leadership. Leading myself became a top priority, so that I could successfully lead others.

One strong reflection on my time leading an organisation is this: the best kind of learning happens on the job. I'm so glad I put my hand up before I was totally ready, as I got such a valuable education. It fast-tracked my development as a leader and broadened what I can offer others.

be your best self

Do you view yourself as a leader? Answer the two questions we posed earlier. Write your answers down so you can properly reflect, come back to them and refine.

- Why do you want to lead? (What do you have to offer and what is your leadership purpose?)

- Why should you lead? (How would you inspire and create conditions where others can be their best?)

WINNING PLAYS

- YOU DON'T NEED AN EXPENSIVE COURSE OR AN MBA TO BE A GREAT LEADER. NOR DO YOU NEED TO WAIT FOR AN OPPORTUNITY. THERE ARE TONS OF WAYS TO DEVELOP AND DEMONSTRATE YOUR LEADERSHIP CAPACITY RIGHT NOW. NO PERMISSION REQUIRED.

- LEADING IS A MIXTURE OF MANAGING YOURSELF AND LEADING OTHERS. IN THAT ORDER.

- BEING FIT TO LEAD IMPROVES YOUR CHANCES OF SUCCESS.

- BAD LEADERSHIP IS EVERYWHERE, WHICH GIVES YOU THE OPPORTUNITY TO DO IT DIFFERENTLY, TO STAND OUT AND HAVE AN IMPACT. SO THREE CHEERS TO BAD BOSSES!

CHAPTER 8

BUILDING YOUR LEADERSHIP CONFIDENCE

The person who risks nothing, DOES NOTHING.

Leadership confidence comes from how you feel about yourself as a leader, and how you are able to use all your experiences – good and bad – to learn and develop.

TAKE EVERY OPPORTUNITY TO LEAD

Expand your thinking about what leadership is. You can lead yourself, others, and projects. You don't need to have a team of people to be a true leader. Have you ever spoken up in a meeting when everyone else remained quiet? That's leadership. Have you helped someone who was struggling? That's leadership. Made a call in your own life that you know is right for you? That's leadership. Stayed behind to do the dirty work while everyone else went home? That's leadership.

MEETINGS ARE WHERE THE LEADERSHIP GAME IS PLAYED

Most of us would say that our workplaces have too many meetings. Opportunities to show what you're made of can be limited and meetings are the one place where you can demonstrate your leadership capacity. You can write all the reports and do all the projects you want, but who holds the real power and status will be made clear in meetings.

We are not suggesting it is easy to speak up, particularly if you are in an environment where your voice is easily drowned out. But you have to try. Take every opportunity to make a contribution in meetings, from volunteering to giving presentations and asking relevant questions, to being well prepared.

THE RIGHT ATTITUDE

Your attitude defines what kind of leader you will become. Do you see opportunities or just the stuff that is wrong? What do you do when things don't go to plan?

Think about what your beliefs around leadership are. Do you think it is about giving orders and exercising control? What are your experiences of leadership and how have they shaped your beliefs?

A leader's attitude is contagious. So what is your team picking up or putting down?

FEEDBACK

Giving feedback

It's not easy; we totally get it. You weren't taught how to give feedback at school. But it's a skill that will be so useful in your professional life. Instead of cringing when you need to do it, make a plan and deliver it with confidence.

Tips on giving feedback:

▲ Tune in to how the other person responds to feedback. Their needs might be different to yours.

▲ Always base your feedback on something doable – make it constructive for both of you.

▲ Think about the key message you want them to take away and structure the conversation around that. Don't fluff about for half an hour before getting to the point.

▲ All your feedback should be about them achieving their goals – not yours.

▲ Be positive. Don't attack them, but base your feedback around a solution.

▲ Consider how you're feeling and if you've chosen the right time to be giving feedback. When you are angry or tired things can come out the wrong way. Choose the right time to get the best result.

Receiving feedback

Ensure you're in the right frame of mind to receive feedback. You need to be prepared to have an open, curious mind and be able to process thoughts and opinions that will potentially differ from your own.

Feedback is a free
education to excellence.
Seek it with sincerity and
receive it with grace.

– ANN MARIE HOUGHTAILING

Tips on receiving feedback:

▲ Choose someone you trust and respect to give it to you.

▲ Know what kind of feedback you are after — help the person to help you.

▲ Listen, listen, listen. Concentrate on what is being said and don't get defensive.

▲ Be aware of your emotions, reactions and body language during the conversation.

▲ Even if you don't agree with the feedback initially, promise yourself that you will take it on board and think about it. If something has surprised or shocked you, you will need time to digest it. Ask them if you can come back and clarify anything you might need to at a later stage, and thank them for their gift (yes, feedback is definitely a gift).

Bianca's Story

During my sporting career, constant feedback was everywhere, whether I liked it or not. I learned pretty quickly I either had to listen or get left behind.

When I first made the Aussie team, I was only 18. All of a sudden, I was surrounded by feedback from everyone: the strength and conditioning coaches on my fitness; the dietician on what foods to eat; and the coach on how I played and how I could get better. My teammates also gave me feedback and expected me to contribute by giving them feedback as well. There is so much to take in, especially when you're the new kid on the block!

Over the years I certainly embraced it; I didn't have much choice. The most successful teams seemed to be flooded with people who could accept feedback and move on. It was very rarely presented as a personal attack, but it was still overwhelming at times.

I tried to explain some of the harsher feedback to friends outside of my athlete's bubble, but it was impossible for them to relate. So I discovered the best way for me to take on the feedback was to not share it with people who wouldn't understand. I didn't need everyone weighing in on what was, ultimately, up to me.

Sport is a unique world, and I am so thankful I played a team sport, as I'm not sure I would have loved having to go through all the ups and downs on my own. It was comforting to know that most feedback was given because the girls, coaches, or whoever, wanted me to be a better player. Who doesn't want that?

Now I crave feedback to the point that I feel a bit lost if I don't have people telling me what they need from me and how I might be better at whatever I'm doing.

Don't get me wrong – I'm not after all the positive fluffy reinforcement all the time, just genuine honesty. I've found this is a big game changer for me as I leave behind my playing career and navigate the real world where people don't offer up as much feedback.

There really is a big wide world out there that exists outside the athlete's bubble!

Initially, receiving constant feedback was really challenging. I struggled to cope with everyone having something to say about me and my performance. But, now, I'm so grateful I had to learn the art of receiving feedback. It made me much tougher.

PRACTICE

Practice makes perfect. We have all heard that a million times but there is so much truth to it (aside from the perfect part, sorry, that won't happen).

When we rehearse or practise something over and over again, our mind and body become more aware of, and more at ease with the action, which then starts to occur naturally.

> Take risks: if you win, you will be happy; if you lose, you will be wise.
>
> – ANONYMOUS

Think about something you have wanted to be better at. It could be a sporting skill, speed-reading, painting, driving or public speaking. Whatever it is, the process of improving always starts off hard and is frustrating. Over time and with repetition it gets easier and far more enjoyable, until you become almost addicted to the quest to conquer the skill.

The same goes for your determination to become a better leader. You gain more confidence in your ability after you practise something, and leadership is no different. When a leader displays confidence in a skill or an idea they are presenting, they signal to the people around them that they are doing a good job or that the idea is a sound one.

VISUALISATION

The more we rehearse something, whether that be physically or mentally, or through visualisation, the better we are at eliminating the fear that comes with doing something new. Athletes constantly use visualisation to prepare themselves. Seeing is believing. If they can see themselves executing something well, they are halfway to making it happen. Athletes also consider all the what-ifs to make sure they are prepared for when things don't go to plan.

Similarly, you will have a hugely confident team if you, as their leader, have visualised success and properly prepared by considering all the possible what-ifs in your action plan.

TAKING RISKS

Practice and taking risks go hand in hand when it comes to accomplishing what we want to achieve. The more you practise taking risks by putting your hand up to lead, the easier it will become.

Taking risks is scary for everyone. The key to it, like with most things, is to change your mindset. Reframe what the risk means to you by seeing it as a gateway to success, rather than a roadblock.

When we thought about writing a book it scared the life out of both of us. Neither of us knew exactly how we were going to do it, but we kept asking ourselves, what is the worst thing that could happen? In the end, it was all about our attitude. We wanted to give it a go, despite knowing there was potential for us to fail.

It is one thing to weigh up the risk and go for it, it's another to be blasé. You've got to find a balance between the risk and reward, and be prepared for what will happen if the risk doesn't come off. You have a book in your hands, so we pulled this one off!

Leading from the front is critical to a successful outcome. Weigh up the pros and cons and gain the respect of your team by having the confidence and determination to take a risk.

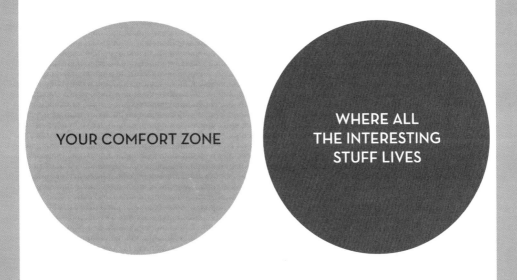

be your best self

Approach one or two people in your world who you trust and respect, and ask them to give you feedback on something you consider important to helping you reach a goal. You don't want to seek feedback from the 'cheerleaders' in your life, but rather the people who will be able to say it like it is.

How did this make you feel? Did you understand the feedback? Take the necessary steps to make the adjustments you need.

WINNING PLAYS

- MEETINGS GIVE YOU AN OPPORTUNITY TO SHOW WHAT YOU HAVE TO OFFER. USE THEM TO DEMONSTRATE YOUR CAPACITY.

- A LEADER'S ATTITUDE IS CRITICAL. CHOOSE WISELY.

- FEEDBACK IS THE STUFF OF CHAMPIONS. INVITE IT, ACCEPT IT, AND USE IT AS DATA TO MOVE TOWARDS BEING THE BEST YOU CAN BE.

- REHEARSAL BUILDS LEADERSHIP CONFIDENCE.

- YOUR APPETITE FOR RISK DETERMINES WHETHER YOU WILL GIVE SOMETHING A GO – OR NOT. CHECK IN TO SEE IF YOUR COMFORT ZONE IS BIGGER THAN IT NEEDS TO BE.

CHAPTER 9
TEAMWORK

> Alone we can do so little; together we can do so much.
>
> – HELEN KELLER

Being part of a team can look and feel very different for all of us. You probably don't realise how many teams you are directly or indirectly involved in. You might be part of a sports team, but groups at work and families also count as teams.

Sometimes it's hard not to wonder why some teams accomplish very little, while others achieve so much. From our experiences, there is no magic solution; the reality is a strong team is the sum of many parts. Not everything has to be perfect though – remember, perfection is impossible. The ability to quickly and efficiently work through the highs and the lows with each other goes a long way to helping the process.

In successful sporting teams, every individual involved works equally hard. This includes the players themselves and all of the support staff, coaches, medical staff, etc. Genuine team players who focus their efforts on bringing out the best in people, and who take on specific roles while acting and behaving in a suitable way, are key in successful teams. Team performance, not the individual, has to be paramount.

A high-performance team needs the following:

1. A GOOD PLAN

This needs to be solid, simple and easy to follow for all in the team. Everyone needs to have a clear understanding of what the team is aiming for.

2. THE RIGHT PEOPLE

A successful team needs to have specifically skilled people who have the ability to carry out their role under pressure, and have awareness of their own strengths and limitations.

3. CLEAR UNDERSTANDING OF EXPECTATIONS

Everyone's specific role, why they are there and what success looks like all need to be clear. Then it's about bringing the group together to decide what behaviours are expected from one another, how the team wants to operate and what the consequences are if the behaviours are not displayed.

4. STRONG RELATIONSHIPS

Relationships are the key to making it all work. Take the time to get to know each other as people first, and as colleagues second. To build strong relationships in a team, everyone needs to understand how members operate under pressure, how they react to stress and the environment that is best for each individual.

5. OPEN CONVERSATIONS

A team culture that allows and supports genuine conversations is one of the hardest parts to foster. Team members all need to have a voice; be able to share concerns and thoughts; provide encouragement; and give and receive feedback. This won't happen quickly, it will take time.

Bianca's story

You always hear coaches say that the team comes first but I never really knew if everyone in the team actually, truly, believed it.

In all the teams I've been part of, I've come to realise that the notion of team-first means different things to different people. There are some who give everything, no matter what the circumstances, and others who purely focus on personal success. They are two extremes, but it's a fine line and it can be hard to get the balance right. As an athlete, you have to push yourself individually to make a team, then, having been selected, switch to playing your role within the group.

In the latter part of my career, I started to fully appreciate how well a team can work together when the culture is right. In the Aussie Diamonds from 2012 onwards, we worked with leadership specialists who helped us create an environment of trust, respect, understanding and a set of behaviours that would lead us to be as prepared as possible heading into the 2014 Commonwealth Games.

I have been part of teams that have gone down this path before, but this time it was different. Laura Geitz, Kimberlee Green and I were selected by the group to lead the team. After my rollercoaster ride as a player, I'd finally come back into the team and appreciated being there more than ever before, so I was pretty passionate about making it work. I wanted to make sure I gave the team everything I had in order to get that gold medal in Glasgow – something the Diamonds hadn't been able to do since 2002.

Maybe it was divine timing, or perhaps my experience playing in teams and my understanding of what a strong culture actually is came together, but the more I focused on the team and not myself, the better I played.

I was Vice Captain, had worked my way into the starting seven and was playing the best international netball of my life during the 2013 Constellation Cup. I was enjoying playing more than ever, but it came at a price for my aging body.

I had this unique and random moment of clarity after our last test match in 2013 where we beat New Zealand by one goal to win the series. I had played nearly every quarter in five test matches over two weeks. I got back to the hotel, could hardly walk, and just sat in the shower. I was so physically and mentally exhausted from what I had just been through. I couldn't stop crying and it wasn't because I was upset or sad – I just had to let go. I was thoroughly exhausted – in body and mind. It had been a big few months with some amazing highs, but all the hard work and team stuff took its toll on and off the court. It was there and then that I promised myself I was only going to play for another six months.

The Vixens had such a huge year in 2014. We won the premiership and loved every second of that season because we finally had the right mix of youth and experience. We prioritised the team over everything else.

Of course it was no surprise to me how bad my body felt after it all though. We went straight into Commonwealth Games prep and I was finding it harder, but not impossible. We got to Glasgow and I managed to play OK by my standards and had opportunities, but I wasn't really able to play how I wanted to. I ended up out of the starting seven and it was tough to take, especially because I knew I was retiring from the Aussie team at the end (no-one else knew at that stage). The thing is though, I accepted the fact I was on the bench, and that I had to play my role. I knew everyone around me was trying to figure out how I was coping, but I can confidently say, I was okay with it. In the past being benched was something that embarrassed me, but I just knew this time that my main role within that team was to be a leader, to be there to support Geitzy and the rest of the girls, and the reality was, I could do that from the bench. We hadn't spent three years getting the team to where it was for me to be a negative influence on the girls. Kim Green ended up in the same position as me – two out of the three in the leadership group sat on the bench for the gold medal game. It wasn't ideal, but it wasn't about us; it was the best thing for the team. We all walked away with a gold medal knowing everyone in that team (players and support staff) had given everything they had.

LEADING YOUR TEAM

'Lead by example.' We're not sure who owns that phrase, but they were onto something big. Every single day, you should be aiming to lead through your actions. You need to be willing and able to step up and demand that people meet the expectations that have been set, while modelling them yourself. You need to live and breathe the agreed culture.

We have mentioned it before, but it's important to show your vulnerabilities as a leader. No-one is perfect, so if you make a mistake and are unsure about how to navigate everyone eyeballing you for an answer, put your hand up and say you aren't sure. It's not a sign of weakness; it's showing everyone you are human.

We've also mentioned before how important it is to have a relationship with every member of your team, but finding ways to do this without it seeming like a forced assignment can be tough. Being around your team in everyday life is advantageous, as is getting a clear picture of how the world at their level works. If you manage your team sitting at a desk away from everyone else, or only knowing the role you play, then you may struggle to know your group in a real and meaningful way.

beyond the CV

Some ideas to implement to help you get to know your team better:

- Staff days or conferences that are fun, interactive and stimulating for all

- Social activities away from work

- Weekly competitions, incentives or challenges for staff

- Consistent team meetings

- One-on-ones where you spend more time listening than talking.

The environment you create has a huge impact on how valued your team feels and how productive they will be in their roles.

An inspiring workplace

Carolyn Creswell from Carman's Fine Foods is one amazing businesswoman. She bought a muesli business for $1000 in 1992. Add some seriously hard work and quite a few years, and her products are now a permanent fixture in Australian supermarkets. The hard work isn't surprising, but what stands out is the emphasis she puts on making sure the culture of her business is strong, empowering and enjoyable for all of her staff.

She has an office in Melbourne with 20 or so staff, and they meet for lunch every day. She hires someone to come in and heat up everyone's meals and get lunch ready, so the team AND CAROLYN can have some quality time together. Every few weeks she gets someone in to wash her staff members' cars to save them having to do it on their weekends. She provides a kids room and desk so staff can bring their kids to work if they are sick and have a space away from others to care for them and continue working. She allows staff to arrange working hours around their personal commitments such as picking kids up from school.

TIPS ON COMMUNICATING TO LEAD YOUR TEAM EFFECTIVELY

▲ Know what you're talking about. Be clear when talking to the group, and keep referring everything back to the big picture and make sure it links with the 'why' of your team.

▲ Be real. Everything you say should be genuine, relatable and come from a place of honest care and compassion.

▲ Stay humble. Don't act like a big dog. It's not about you; it's not a competition between you and the others, you are all in it together. Don't forget that.

▲ Shut up and listen. Take time to actively listen, and understand others' opinions without interrupting them or swaying the conversation. You'll be surprised how much you will learn.

▲ Know your audience. Think about the language you use. Do you often swear when you speak? Will that offend anyone? Are you using terminology or words that people don't understand? It's important to make sure you cater for everyone in the team. Create an environment where people feel comfortable to ask for clarification.

▲ It's not just about the words. Body language, actions and behaviours are powerful. Be conscious of how you stand, sit and gesture, and where you look. The way you choose to use your body tells the group a powerful story.

be your best self

Think about the team you are currently in or leading …

- Brainstorm what you think the leader should look like. How do they behave, how do they look, what attributes do they have? You are not aiming for perfection, but a good snapshot of the must-haves in effective team leadership.

- We have never heard anyone fess up to being a poor communicator. Usually the finger is pointed elsewhere. Check in with your personal communication skills and style, and get some feedback to ensure you know what works, and what doesn't.

WINNING PLAYS

- KNOW YOUR TEAM, NOT JUST SUPERFICIALLY. TAKE THE TIME TO KNOW EVERY PERSON YOU WORK WITH ON A DAILY BASIS. IF YOU HAVE LARGE NUMBERS, MAKE SURE EVERYONE HAS A TOUCH POINT TO A MANAGER THAT KNOWS THEM WELL.

- IF THEY ARE NOT ON THE BUS, AS A LEADER YOU SHOULD UNDERSTAND WHY THEY'RE NOT HAPPY AND WHAT YOU CAN DO ABOUT IT. SUPPORT THEM AS BEST YOU CAN.

- YOUR SUCCESS IN A TEAM IS ENTIRELY DEPENDENT ON OTHERS. AIM TO MANAGE YOUR ATTITUDE AND YOUR CAPACITY TO CREATE AND SUSTAIN THE ENVIRONMENT OTHERS NEED TO THRIVE.

you're got this

being your best self: nailing the career and the life you want

To help you nail a BIG life, we have some more things for you to think about on your journey to reaching your version of success. We want you to think about what kind of life you have and what you want it to be. By getting passionate and getting sorted you will be able to kick butt on your career and life journey. We have been encouraging you to think about your version of success the whole way through this book. Now it's time to focus on what YOU want to achieve and how YOU are going to get yourself there.

We have had the warm up; we are now about to take to the court. Ready to play?

> You've got to take the initiative and play your game. In a decisive set, confidence is the difference.
>
> – CHRIS EVERT

CHAPTER 10
WHERE ARE YOU HEADING?

Define success on your own terms, achieve it by your own rules, and build a life you're proud to live.

– ANNE SWEENEY

When people come for career coaching, they often look to us as experts. The first thing we say is that they hold the answers; we don't have a crystal ball. With a somewhat confused look on their face, they listen and probably wonder what they are paying us for. But there isn't any point in us acting like experts, because we are not. They are. You are.

DEFINING YOUR VERSION OF SUCCESS

Real success starts with defining it in your own terms. It's the first thing you need to tackle when you are thinking about where you want to go, because your definition will dictate the path you take. But defining what success means to you doesn't happen by chance; you've got to do the work. Reflect, pay attention and tune in to those thoughts that you are too afraid to say out loud. Dream up what a big life would look like for you. Some people steer away from using the word 'dreams', likening them to fantasies. And they probably will be fantasies if you don't do anything about them. Think of dreams as calls to action. Your dreams are made up of your purpose, your passion and the stuff that you can't stop thinking about. Dreaming big then defining success for yourself gives you a plan worth working towards.

What are your beliefs about success?

When it comes to success, nothing matters more than your beliefs. What do you believe? Do you think that success only happens for a chosen few, or lucky people, or that there is a time frame for it? Do you believe that every situation is an opportunity to learn or that there are failures and successes, and nothing in between? Do you believe past experiences predict future ones? Beliefs define your reality. What reality are you choosing for yourself?

What is your definition of success?

We were taught to worry about what we wanted to do when we grew up, so it's no wonder that when we start to focus on defining success for ourselves, job titles are the first place our minds go. We want you to dig deeper than that and define who you want to *be* rather than what you want to *do*. The being comes before the doing.

Try the following exercise to define your version of success:

▲ What do you want your life to look like? Where are you, who are you with, what are you doing? Write your vision down.

▲ Note down every belief you have about success. Make sure they are things you really believe, not just things you have got used to telling yourself (or picked up from others).

▲ List the things you are currently doing that honour your vision of how you want your life to be, as well as the things that are not helping. Starting today, what do you need to start or stop?

▲ Turn all your notes into a paragraph titled, 'My definition of success right now'. Set a reminder in your phone to revisit this paragraph in a year's time to see if your definition has changed.

Your definition of success can (and should) change

What is important to you when you're 20 may not be so important when you're 40. Your definition can change over time, particularly as you learn more about yourself and what you are truly capable of. Be flexible enough to recognise opportunity (don't say no to something because it doesn't fit your rigid criteria) but know your core non-negotiables.

And while the meaning of success can change for you over time, having a definition of it gives you an anchor point. Your definition then acts as a filter to determine whether you are on the right path or not. This can be challenging, as others may try to encourage you down different paths, but remember that you own your definition; they have no claim on it.

Bianca's Story

I spent 17 years playing netball at the elite level. What success looked like to me five years ago is so different to what it looks like now. I had such belief in my ability as a player and leader, that all I wanted was to win a premiership with the Vixens, get myself into the team for the Commonwealth Games and win a gold medal. No big deal. Why not aim high?

After I retired from playing in June 2015, every second person asked 'what are you going to do now?' It was like I had died and they were asking how I could possibly be reborn and have a happy and successful life. Little do people understand that even though it might look pretty incredible being an athlete from the outside, I assure you, on the inside, it's not always like that.

The advantage of being a female athlete in Australia then was that we weren't paid as full-time athletes (yes, I'm saying that it was an advantage), so I had to have something else. I went to uni, tried my hand at being a PE and Science teacher, I worked at Essendon Football Club in the community division (that's where I met Leigh) and started my own businesses all while playing for my country. I count myself lucky that when I retired my whole world wasn't over. Many full-time athletes have to start again upon retirement as they aren't given the time to study (or don't have the self-motivation to make it happen for themselves).

By the time I finally committed to walking off the court for good, I was mentally so excited to start the next phase. Success had changed from winning games and gold medals to being able to create a life that I wanted. I didn't want to go and get a full-time job working for someone else, I wanted to utilise my entrepreneurial brain to make the most of the brand I had created during my netball career. I also wanted to have a go at commentating, provide opportunities for young girls through my own netball academy, work with the Netball Players Association and pursue other business opportunities. And, of course, I wanted to write a book … this one! Tick.

Being an athlete is a seriously selfish business (and so it should be). You have to commit all of yourself to it. I love the fact that I don't have to live that way anymore, and that I can spend more time with my family and friends where it isn't all about me (although my sisters probably disagree). Yes, it's risky to live off lots of random projects, and I know not everyone can relate (I see the confusion on people's faces when they ask what I do now), but I'm living out my dreams and doing what I love to do.

My definition of success has changed too. And I know my new path won't always be easy to take. I already wake up some days and want to just get one secure job, but I quickly realise that I don't want to live my life that way. I feel prepared that if something doesn't work out or go to plan, I have the power to change my plan of attack. Like a particular person always asks me … 'What's the worst thing that could happen?'. Leigh Russell (on my Board of Directors – see p. 170) is always right … damn it!

PICTURING SUCCESS

Writing down your goals is one thing, but actually visualising your goals can be really powerful too. It's also much easier than remembering to revisit written goals.

Vision boards are a great way of reflecting on who you are and where you want to head. They are really simple to make: just get together some images, words and photos that inspire you. The idea behind them is that when you surround yourself with images of your intentions (the future self or life you want), your awareness, passion and activity are sparked because your mind responds strongly to visual stimulation. So in other words, you are helping your brain help yourself.

Vision boards are everywhere but yours is unique to you.

Getting started

We both tackle vision boards in different ways. Try the approach that suits you best.

Collect a bunch of images from magazines, some cardboard (or something similar) and glue. You might also want to look for images you like on Instagram, Pinterest or Google Images. Print them out and add them to your board. By doing it this way you can display it around your house, in your study, or anywhere you can regularly look at it. I took a picture of mine and use it as the background image on my phone.

SAY yes
& figure it out
AFTERWARDS

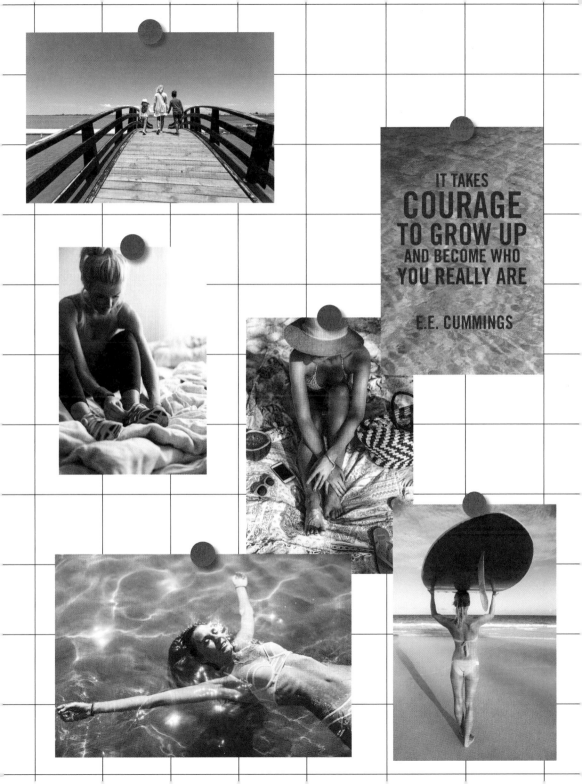

IT TAKES
COURAGE
TO GROW UP
AND BECOME WHO
YOU REALLY ARE

E.E. CUMMINGS

I'm all about the digital world. So get Googling and find images of things you love. Instagram and Pinterest are good places to look. Find accounts you like, or search for inspirational hashtags. Cut and past your images into a PowerPoint document or similar. You can then save it as a jpeg file and use it as your desktop picture on your computer, or print it out and put it somewhere you will see often. That way, it's always there to remind you of your vision.

Believe

YOU GET WHAT YOU SETTLE FOR

FEEL THE
FEAR
AND
DO IT
ANYWAY

Tips on creating your board:

▲ This is the time to set your fears aside. As you are flipping through images, rip out (or print out) things that you are attracted to. You don't need to know why at this stage – just collect anything that jumps out. Cut out pictures, words, poetry and phrases (you could even draw something if that is your thing). Getting enough material may take some time and you might need to look in a few different places.

▲ If you're having trouble starting, chunk your thinking into these areas:

- Career and business

- Personal and family

- Health and wellness

- Bucket list dreams.

▲ When you find yourself saying, 'yes, that is me', or 'that is what I want to do', this is a sign that you're choosing the right things. If it speaks to you, collect it. The images should be visual representations of your aspirations and dreams, big or small.

▲ Think about all the topics we have covered. Go back through some of the notes you have made about who you are and where you want to go. Collect some material that speaks to that.

▲ If you are feeling stuck, think about what would be on your anti-vision board. What kinds of images, quotes, etc. would represent what you don't want to be? Or what are things that don't make you feel good? Thinking this through might help you get clear about some of the things that *are* meaningful to you.

▲ Lay your images out on your board before you glue (or before you save your PowerPoint as an image). You may want to group things into the areas we discussed above or just go for it. It's normal for this part to take ages – just try a few things and let it flow.

▲ Get as creative as you want. Some people go over the top of their images with a sealer or with stickers, glitter or stamps, etc.

Inspirational reminder

Once you are finished, put your board somewhere where you will see it every day. Use it as a reminder, or as inspiration, to check in with your progress towards your goals, or to figure out which area to work on next.

Do what inspires you, but some tricks to help you along include:

▲ Look at it last thing at night and first thing in the morning.

▲ Nut out a plan to move your life or career towards each of the areas on your board one by one. The idea is not to feel overwhelmed by your goals, but to move, bit by bit, in the direction you want to go.

▲ Tune in to your mindset. Having the belief that you can get there, and visualising yourself doing it are both important.

▲ Don't forget to celebrate goals as you reach them, and acknowledge any changes you make that will move you towards accomplishing more.

YOUR INNER MENTOR

Just as we have an inner critic, we also have an inner mentor. It's the part of you that is wise and pays no attention to the 'shoulds' and negative comparisons. The inner mentor is often hard to really hear – sometimes the volume on the critic is much louder than the mentor (particularly if the critic has been talking for a very long time). But you can use your inner mentor to help you develop a vision for your life and career, make decisions and define your version of success.

Don't get us wrong, external opinions are important for a whole range of practical reasons (see p. 172). But your inner mentor also needs a seat at the table. Besides, your inner mentor is always available and ready to help, never too busy and knows you extremely well. She keeps it simple and doesn't overcomplicate situations.

Your inner mentor helps you to look at your life from a different perspective, dial down the noise from the critic and get clear on what is important. In the same way we ask older people, 'what advice would you give your 18-year-old self?' to learn from their wisdom, we can use our inner mentor to help us shape our future.

How to tap your inner mentor

The following task is a visualisation exercise[6], so you will need about 20 minutes and a notebook and pen. Don't like visualisation or think it is a bit soft? Don't write it off yet, stay curious and give it a go. Visualisation techniques are a proven tool for athletes – studies have shown they make a big difference to performance[7]. The simple act of visualising your future helps you create present conditions to get there.

1. FIND SOMEWHERE COMFY TO SIT.

Focus on your breathing by slowing it down and breathing deeply.

2. IMAGINE YOURSELF LEAVING YOUR BODY,

floating above yourself. Observe yourself and your life as it is today.

3. GO FORWARD 20 YEARS AND MEET YOUR SUCCESSFUL FUTURE SELF.

Where is she? Who is with her? What kind of place does she live in? How does it feel to walk around in her shoes?

4. OBSERVE YOUR FUTURE SELF. WHAT DOES SHE LOOK LIKE?

How is she dressed? What do you notice most strongly about her? What is she like now she has succeeded in everything she has dreamed of doing?

5. HAVE A CONVERSATION WITH YOUR FUTURE SELF. WHAT DOES SHE SAY TO YOU?

What advice does she have for you? Ask her questions like, 'what do I need to know to get from where I am now to where you are?' or any other question you might need answered.

6. WHAT DOES YOUR FUTURE SELF WANT YOU TO DO?

To remember? To focus on? What is important to your future self?

7. WHEN YOU ARE FINISHED TALKING,

come back to the present. Make some notes about what your future self told you, how you felt and what you need to do differently to create the future you want. Does it change your priorities? Make some things clearer?

You don't need to do a full visualisation exercise every time you want to tap the resources of your inner mentor. Keep her in mind as you go about your daily life. If you are feeling like you could benefit from hearing from a mentor, you can always quickly tap into the resources within yourself.

be your best self

Now you are at the end of the chapter, give it a skim read and pick the activity that will have an impact for you right now (you can come back to the rest). Or navigate to the activity that most appeals to you with this handy list:

- What is in your definition of success? (p. 133)
- Picturing success (vision board) (p. 136)
- How to tap your inner mentor (p. 144)

WINNING PLAYS

- YOUR BELIEFS ABOUT SUCCESS DETERMINE YOUR SUCCESS.

- YOUR DEFINITION OF SUCCESS CAN AND SHOULD EVOLVE OVER TIME AS YOU DO MORE AND LEARN MORE.

- USING A VISION BOARD CAN HELP YOU CLARIFY WHAT YOU WANT (OR DON'T WANT).

- YOUR INNER MENTOR IS THERE FOR YOU 24/7. TUNE OUT THE NOISE AND TUNE IN TO WHAT THIS WISE WOMAN IS SAYING.

CHAPTER 11
OWN IT

We talked to you about what success truly is in the last chapter, which has hopefully triggered some thoughts for you. Remember, this is not about your friends or family, but you. After thinking about who you really are and where you want to go, you now need to take your success mindset to the next level by completely owning your success.

You have read what we think about the role of luck in success – it is totally overblown. Luck doesn't help you work hard to capitalise on opportunities you might have – it's all you (or not). Owning your success is about acknowledging the things you achieve and do well, and being reasonably comfortable articulating them. We often hear people who have achieved a lot downplay their successes. Too often they will put disclaimers at the end of sentences, particularly if they are uncomfortable with someone pointing out their achievements. Test this out next time you talk to someone about something positive they have done. We bet that they try to convince you that their success is due to external forces (like luck or team effort) rather than internal ones, like ability, effort, knowledge and skill.

DO YOU DESERVE YOUR ACHIEVEMENTS?

You bet you do. But do you really believe it? When you are able to own your success, you have a better chance of repeating it. If you point to external forces like chance or team effort to explain your success, you may feel like it was was a fluke. You might even believe the success is unlikely to be repeated (and that might turn into a self-fulfilling prophecy).

You deserve your accomplishments just as much as your team does. There is always a time to acknowledge the people around you who have made a contribution, but equally, there is a time to acknowledge your role. Always attributing your success to others is a career inhibitor. By empowering yourself to own it – the successes and mistakes – you can take charge of your career and life.

Leigh's Story

Owning success is a very personal topic for me. For many years I struggled to recognise that my success was down to my ability and hard work, rather than luck. After major wins (such as promotions, new roles or projects going really well), I would say things to myself like, *I was in the right place at the right time; I got lucky; I knew the right people; my team is the real reason we were able to be successful; and even, I wonder who their first pick was? Am I just here to be the token chick? When will they find me out?*

These thoughts really plagued me and undermined how I felt about myself. This played out in a couple of ways. First, I was never comfortable about receiving praise for a job well done. I would deflect it and wonder if they truly meant it. Second, I often doubted my decisions – if luck played a part the first time, then I may not succeed the second time.

My inner critic was a loud contributor on these issues. I remember telling my mentors about feeling like I was always waiting for a tap on the shoulder, for someone to say 'the joke is up' and put me back where I 'belonged'. Distancing myself from my achievements was not something that I was ever taught; it was just a mindset that wasn't very helpful.

The penny really dropped for me though when I started working on and talking a lot about personal brand (see p. 154). Taking accountability for who you are, what you think and how you go about it was at the core of my teachings, but here I was, thinking I was a fraud.

Old habits die hard. I had to practise to change my fraud mindset. It was like spitting razor blades the first time I tried to articulate my achievements, but now it comes much more easily. Getting clear about my version of success and celebrating the steps I've taken to get there has really helped me.

BUILDING PERSONAL ACCOUNTABILITY

Owning your success is all about building your personal accountability. It's being prepared to answer for the outcomes of all your behaviours, actions and choices. When you're personally accountable, you stop assigning blame, or 'should-ing', and making excuses. Genuine accountability creates high performance and leaders who inspire others. Put it into practice and see the difference it makes.

It's not what you are that holds you back, it's what you think you are not.

– DENIS WAITLEY

Shake it off!

In order to own your own career success, you need to stop externalising success and start internalising achievements. Shaking off feeling like a fraud and taking accountability for your work takes effort. Try these strategies:

- When others recognise something you have done, 'thank you' can be a complete sentence. You don't need to put a disclaimer at the end. Likewise, watch for disclaimers in the things you say to yourself. This might take some practice.

- Keep your inner critic at a healthy distance. Use the critic to be thorough, rather than doubtful or dismissive.

- Make sure there are not two groups of successes in your head: so-called real successes and the ones that don't count. This is why tuning in to your own version of success is so important; you can easily define what is real and not. (Hint: it's all real.)

- If you are feeling like a fraud and finding it difficult to own your successes, ask yourself, *what will it take to feel successful?* How many times do you need to do something to feel it, and is that reasonable?

- Sing your own praises. Don't wait for others to do it, because while you are waiting, opportunity sails by. Get clear on what your talents and triumphs are, and make sure the people who need to know, know. This might mean using meetings differently, or having different types of conversations and using them to your advantage. Be strategic, but find a way.

be your best self

List two or three significant successes from the last couple of years. Now list two or three more recent successes (they don't have to be big). Did you own each one, or write them off? What would you do next time to own your success?

Success is all about the feeling as much as the action. What will it take for you to *feel* successful? How will you know you have been successful when you get there?

The next time someone praises you or compliments your success, say 'thank you', and end the sentence there. Don't add any disclaimers or attribute it to external forces. Just 'thank you'.

WINNING PLAYS

- YOU DESERVE YOUR ACCOMPLISHMENTS. WE BELIEVE IT – DO YOU?

- FEELING LIKE A FRAUD IS COMMON BUT STOPS YOU FROM RECOGNISING YOUR ACHIEVEMENTS. IT'S OK TO BE PROUD OF WHAT YOU HAVE DONE. GET CLEAR ON WHAT IT WILL TAKE TO FEEL SUCCESSFUL SO YOU CAN OWN YOUR OWN SUCCESS.

- OWNING YOUR SUCCESS MEANS YOU HAVE A BETTER CHANCE OF BEING ABLE TO REPEAT IT.

- BUILDING PERSONAL ACCOUNTABILITY BUILDS YOUR BRAND (SEE P. 150).

CHAPTER 12
BUILDING YOUR BRAND

Life isn't about finding yourself. Life is about creating yourself.
– GEORGE BERNARD SHAW

Have a flick through your cupboards and look around your home. Think about some of the big brands you have chosen to include in your life. What is it that you love about them? What makes them stand out from the rest of the market? If the marketers have done their job properly, you love certain brands over others because there is an expectation of quality, of superior benefits, or an experience you can't get elsewhere.

Personal branding employs the same concepts. It is based on the value proposition we bring to the table – our unique set of skills, talents, behaviours and values – and is critical to success. A strong personal brand will enable you to forge positive relationships, by drawing in the 'right' kinds of people. It increases your potential to land leadership roles (with a strong and consistent brand, people can understand what they are getting or buying in to), and increases your credibility, which is important for establishing trust: the cornerstone of leadership.

Your personal brand tells your audience four things: who you are, what you do, what you stand for and what makes you stand out. The challenge is that while most of us don't think strategically or consciously about our brand, it is the one thing that is either helping or hindering our careers. Your brand is the stuff of conversations when you are out of the room. We all have conversations about the impact of others on us, particularly our leaders – *I just don't have a good feeling about her* or *she doesn't realise the effect she has on her staff*, for example. The 'water cooler' conversation is inevitable. What will they be saying about you?

When I was a teenager, basketball was my passion. I was obsessed with anything to do with Michael Jordan and desperately wanted a pair of 'Jordan 5s'. My family weren't in a financial position to buy these shoes for me, so I went and got myself a job, saved for a couple months (they were ridiculously expensive, even back then) and bought the shoes. I still remember the day I put them on my feet and how they made me feel. In hindsight, I believed they made me part of the 'cool kids' club and, of course, would make me play better basketball. I wasn't consciously thinking these things at the time, but I had definitely put a premium on the brand and what it meant to me.

In reality, these shoes would not have cost a great deal to make. They didn't make me fly higher or run any faster, but none of that mattered to me at the time; I was buying into part of a powerful brand. It was emotional, not rational, which is exactly what the concept of branding is all about.

PERSONAL BRAND – IT'S ALL ABOUT THE LITTLE BIG THINGS

So, what does a personal brand consist of?

Your brand blueprint

Being sure of what is important to you – your non-negotiables in life – is an essential building block of your brand. Knowing your values means you can use them as signposts in your decision-making processes. If something is consistent with your values, you might consider it. If it isn't, it should be disregarded.

The second part of the blueprint is to check that your behaviours match your values. Talking the talk, but not walking the walk is a brand killer. Think of the last time you called a company, only to find yourself on hold, listening to a recorded voice tell you that you are a valued customer. After a while, you start to question the truthfulness of this statement (their behaviour does not match their words). This can disengage you as a customer or, worse, you might start to badmouth the company based on your experience with them. The same applies to people – behave consistently and in a way that honours what you stand for. When you boil it down, you should have three or four things that you truly value over others. Make these your signposts and shape your behaviours to match.

Your personal appearance

We are calling this one out. Yes, it really does matter. The saying, 'you never get a second chance to make a first impression' is true. Research tells us you have a very short amount of time, less than a second, to make an impression on someone[8]. What you wear and how you use this powerful visual tool forms part of your overall brand message.

Let's be clear – we are addressing this because of how the world is, not how we wish it to be. We wish we were more evolved human beings who could see past what people wear but, the truth is, we can't and it *matters*. And it matters even more for women, who are judged more harshly on their appearance.

However, don't confuse personal appearance with fashion. Paying attention to how you might use this visual brand-builder doesn't mean you should rush out and buy designer gear. It has more to do with using what you have in a way that works for you, in the environment that you are in. Our rule on this is always to dress for the job you want, not the job you have, meaning that we will often dress up rather than down if we are a bit unsure about what to wear.

For you, it might simply mean being more conscious about the messages you are sending with what you wear and how you wear it.

Your competencies

These are your professional skills, including your capacity to be an effective communicator, your emotional intelligence and your technical ability to do your job. The good news? These are all skills that can be learned, practised and refined to help build your brand.

Your self-knowledge

Know your strengths and your opportunities to develop. (Some people call these weaknesses — they are only weaknesses if you are not aware of them.)

The point of brand building is not to be perfect at everything. We are deluding ourselves if we think that is the aim (remember, perfection simply doesn't exist). But having a genuine understanding about what you bring to the table, and equally, what are not areas of strength, are very powerful tools. The only way you can do this, though, is to practise getting comfy with all parts of yourself — warts and all. This means you need to be courageous enough to discover them, and be savvy enough to use the information in a way that helps you, instead of getting bogged down. This isn't easy, but when you know yourself, you are more powerful. Once you know your strengths, you can continue to enhance them and work in areas that showcase them.

Historically, career-coaching techniques demanded clients turn their weaknesses into strengths. But, in practice, a lot of time and energy was spent focusing on weaknesses rather than turning them into strengths.

It's now clear that it's better to work on strengths by honing and finessing them, so they become more and more powerful.

THE BRAND TOOLKIT: THE BREAKERS AND THE BUILDERS

As you read through our brand breakers and builders, work out what you need to start, stop or keep.

Breakers

▲ **Know everything**
You know that person – the one that always says too much at meetings or can't be told anything, thinking they know it all already? Don't be like them; their behaviour is bad for their brand.

▲ **Think no-one is watching**
Time and time again people are caught out when they act in ways that don't correspond with their values or try to get away with something because they believe the focus isn't on them. There is always someone watching and taking notes. Live by the motto, 'would I do it if my grandma (or whoever might be important to you) was watching?'

▲ **Let up once you are 'let in'**
Building a personal brand is a lifelong exercise, not something you do for a short period of time (to get a promotion or spot on the team, for example). Once you get your foot in the door, you have to put even more energy into building your brand. Sports coaches, for example, sometimes act one way

before the title of head coach comes along, only to drop the behaviours that got them there once they are in the new position. It only takes a little time for people to start thinking, *wait a minute, this is not what we signed up for.*

▲ **Be someone you're not**
Ah, it is so easy to say 'just be yourself', isn't it? But we know it's not, particularly in a world where polished social media images and #shinysuccess stories rule supreme. But being someone you are not ultimately sets you up to ruin your brand. It takes a truckload of energy to keep up the façade you create, and you may become a person you don't even recognise. Being yourself doesn't mean you have to let it all hang out, but rather, it's about creating a brand where you don't live in fear that you will be found out.

Builders

▲ **Be a sponge, say yes**
More often than not, people will say no before they say yes. It's habitual, instinctive and safe. Being a sponge to opportunities is an easy way to stand out, even when it scares the hell out of you. Saying yes will push you out of your comfort zone and allow you to demonstrate what you are truly made of. Tina Fey describes this as the 'AHA moment' in her career and how it has helped her keep moving forward:
A couple of times I've been called on to do things – jobs or whatever – where I've felt, maybe I'm not quite ready. Maybe it's a little early for this to happen to me. But the rules are so ingrained. 'Say yes, and you'll figure it out afterward' has helped me to be more adventurous. It has definitely helped me be less afraid[9].
Being a sponge doesn't mean though that you should say yes to everything. It can be strategic, or it can be stupid. A strategic yes is not one that comes because you *can't* say no, it is one that comes *instead* of no.

▲ **Follow your passions**
The easiest way to build your brand is to do something you love doing. People working on something they're passionate about have a brightness in their

eyes and their enthusiasm is infectious. Test this out next time you are having a conversation with someone. Ask them what they dislike doing. Then ask them what they love doing. Observe how their body language, tone of voice and rate of speech changes.

▲ Under promise, over deliver

We can be so caught up in trying to meet expectations that we give ourselves short time frames on which to deliver, often with no 'fat' built in for unexpected events. Personal brand is damaged when you don't deliver on promises (all talk, no action), but it is enhanced when you exceed expectations.

▲ Be willing to fail

One of the great high-performance principles is the willingness to fail. We think this is such an important one we have devoted a whole other chapter to the fear of failure (see page 62). For athletes, the willingness to fail is especially important. We want them to fail and fail often, because we know they will utilise what they learn to improve their performance. Being willing to fail means you won't be focused on the what-ifs, but on asking, 'how can I make this work for me?' You will be curious about the experience, rather than simply seeing it as a loss.

Failure only damages personal brand when you try to hide it. People tend to feel more enraged about a cover-up than a mistake or failure. Getting comfortable with failure actually wins people (and businesses, for that matter) brand-building points.

ße your best self

What is your brand proposition? What makes you stand out?

- List some people you admire with strong personal brands. What is their brand about (what are they known for)?

- What do you think *your* brand is? Describe yourself in three words. You may like to write sentences to begin with, but try to distil them down to three words that mean something to you.

- Ask two or three people to describe you in three words. Are they the same as your three words? If they are different, why do you think that is?

- Think about the words you used to describe yourself. Are they the words of your current brand, or where you want it to be?

- What are the three key messages you want your brand to be about? What do you need to do to maintain it or to bridge the gap (if there is one)? What do you need to stop, start or keep doing?

- List three things you are going to do to start building your brand more consciously.

WINNING PLAYS

- YOU ARE THE CEO OF YOU. YOU CAN CHOOSE A BRAND THAT REFLECTS YOUR UNIQUE TALENTS, SKILLS, VALUES AND BEHAVIOURS.

- PERSONAL BRAND IS WHAT OTHERS SAY ABOUT YOU WHEN YOU HAVE LEFT THE ROOM – MAKE SURE IT IS AN INTERESTING AND POSITIVE CONVERSATION.

- YOUR BRAND IS FOUNDED ON KNOWING WHAT YOUR VALUES ARE. THIS IS YOUR BRAND BLUEPRINT.

- STRONG PERSONAL BRANDS ARE BUILT BY DISPLAYING CONSISTENT BEHAVIOURS OVER TIME. THEY CAN TAKE A LONG TIME TO BUILD, BUT A SHORT TIME TO BE DESTROYED.

CHAPTER 13
TAPPING THE PASSION PIPELINE

Choose a job you
love, and you will
never have to work a
day in your life.

– ANONYMOUS

Now you have had time to think about your brand, it's time to build on that further and work out what you are great at and what you love doing. Some people wait most of their lives before finding those answers. Some are conditioned to meet the expectations of others (for example, someone whose parents were a certain profession might feel an expectation to follow suit). And some are so busy 'doing' that they forget to tap into what is truly important to them.

TRYING TO 'FIND' YOUR PASSION

Are you feeling the pressure to find your passion? Is there a log jam in your head? Stop. Passion isn't something to be found, it is in YOU. Reframe the question from what is your passion to what makes you come alive? What lights a fire in your belly? Put your energy into understanding yourself rather than trawling through a list of possible passions. If you haven't exactly found your sweet spot yet, you are far from alone. But you need to spend some time thinking it through and listening to your inner mentor; the answer won't magically appear.

PASSION TIPS

Passion tip #1: passions are not interests

You can be interested in a whole range of things, from sport, to cooking, to astronomy. You might have a long list of things that interest you, but within that list, just one or two of them will be more meaningful than the others. How can you tell? They will make you feel differently than the other things on the list.

Passion tip #2: your passion is your greatest love story

When we work with people to explore possible passions, we ask them all sorts of questions. During the conversation, there will almost always be a change of body language — their eyes light up, they speak faster, they might even get breathless. Sometimes these cues are not obvious right away. But usually, when someone focuses on something they love, it's obvious — they come alive!

Your life passions should be your greatest loves, the highest expression of who you are and the unique talents you have.

Passion tip #3: your passion lives in YOUR heart

Your passion is YOUR passion, which is really awesome, because the world needs people to be passionate about all sorts of things. What an incredibly boring and one-dimensional place it would be if we were all into the same thing.

Your passion doesn't have to be incredible or impressive; it can be as simple as finding the one thing in life that brings you the most joy. Extraordinary things happen when ordinary people tap into their passions.

Passion tip #4: passion is a key ingredient in being the best you can be

When you work with your passion, great things can happen – your confidence, mindset and results all improve.

Athletes call this 'working with flow' or being in the zone. When they do what they love, they lose track of time and experience effortless concentration and that in-the-moment feeling when nothing else matters. More often than not, when that happens for us non-athletes, it means we are in our passion zone.

Passion tip #5: don't hide behind the belief that others define your ceiling

Only YOU can define your ceiling, or what your limits are. No-one else should try to do this for you. This may be difficult, as your real passion might be very different from what your parents, friends or others want or expect of you. We are often taught to ask permission instead of asking ourselves who we are and where our passion may lie. Getting clear of this can be tough, but living a life full of regret or frustration is tougher still.

Passion tip #6: don't wait for something to smack you in the face

If you are on a journey of passion discovery, don't wait for something to come to you. Sometimes it involves trial and error, but the most important thing is to *do something* to find your passion. Take up a hobby, do a workshop, volunteer, find a little way to dip your toe in the water. There is no 'all or nothing' when it comes to your passion journey. Figure out the excuses you have been making to keep yourself safe and be honest about them (and then talk them through with a mentor or someone on your personal Board of Directors – see p. 170).

The final tip ...

Do it because you can't help it, because if you don't, it will niggle away at you forever. Do it because everything else will feel like a compromise – or someone else's life. That's passion.

Leigh's story

I felt so much pressure to nut out my occupation going into the final years of school. But I really didn't have a clue what I wanted to do. I was interviewed for the paper in year 12 and told them that I wanted to be a federal police officer because 'they get to travel'. I think I just said it to sound cool (I'm not sure that it worked!) but at the time, it just sounded so hollow. So I did a Bachelor of Arts, thinking it would buy me three years to figure out this passion question. I did some really interesting subjects but never came close to feeling like I was in my sweet spot.

I got to the end of the degree and was still a bit lost. By then, I knew in my heart my passion was people. But it seemed so broad and undefined and I wasn't sure about the roles in the career guides that matched 'people'. Besides, I couldn't see how I would live off being passionate about people. So I decided to stay at uni a bit longer and do teaching. My study and teaching experiences showed me, in an even stronger way, that working with people and getting the best out of them was what I loved. But teaching wasn't exactly it for me. So I kept being open to opportunities and moving around. Over time, I found the things that make me come alive by trying things on for size, rather than always having a clear idea. You're lucky if you do have a clear idea, but my coaching work tells me most of us don't start out that way. Some of the things that make me come alive:

- Getting people to think about themselves differently

- Watching someone achieve their goal and knowing I had a role to play

- Working on new solutions to old problems

- Facilitating teams to make change happen

- Writing and presenting.

WHY PEOPLE DON'T FOLLOW THEIR PASSION

People invent all sorts of excuses (dressed up as reasons) to stop themselves tapping their passion. They use the excuses as a shield to avoid thinking about the one or two things that will bring them the most happiness.

If you repeat the excuses often enough, both to yourself and others, it becomes a 'fact'. Do any of these 'facts' sound familiar?

▲ 'Great careers are a matter of luck.'

▲ 'The people who have great careers are not like me, they are smarter (and probably luckier as well).'

▲ 'I would find my passion but I have bills and responsibilities.'

▲ 'I don't have the time.'

▲ 'In the past, I have tried to work it out and didn't get anywhere.'

▲ 'Following passions is a luxury only afforded to some, not me.'

No doubt you could add more to this list.

What are the inner thoughts that are stopping you from following your passion? Don't let yourself off the hook – it is way too important.

be your best self

Life is one big choose-your-own-adventure book. Have you chosen your adventure? Write down anything and everything (little and big) you're interested in doing and being, even the things that seem unattainable or perhaps those things you have only whispered to yourself. Use the passion tips in this chapter to get creative.

Reduce the list to just a few things by identifying the things that make you come alive.

How might you make these things a part of your life if they are not currently part of what you do?

WINNING PLAYS

- PASSIONS ARE NOT OUT THERE, THEY ARE INSIDE YOU. SOMETIMES YOU HAVE TO LISTEN HARD AND SPEND TIME REFLECTING ON WHAT TRULY LIGHTS A FIRE IN YOUR BELLY.

- PASSION WILL HELP YOU BE THE BEST VERSION OF YOU. WHEN YOU ARE PASSIONATE ABOUT WHAT YOU DO, IT IS OBVIOUS.

- DON'T WAIT. YOU HAVE TO DO SOMETHING TO TAP YOUR PASSIONS. PASSIONS DON'T JUST SNEAK UP ON YOU AND SMACK YOU IN THE FACE.

CHAPTER 14

CREATING THE BOD

One thing we have noticed about women with lofty goals: they often try to go it alone. They keep what is going on in their lives and careers to themselves, maintaining a façade that says all is OK. They might find it difficult to let people in, ask for help or others' opinions, based on any number of the fears we have covered in *Game On*. For them, having all the answers, all of the time becomes some sort of badge of honour.

However, you really only need to scratch the surface of these professional lives to see things are often far from optimal. In fact, doing it alone could be the worst career strategy ever.

THE BOD

One of the best, most game-changing pieces of advice we can give (because it has been so powerful for both of us and everyone we know who adopts this strategy), is to create a personal board of directors, or BOD. You may have heard of boards in the corporate sense – a group of people charged with the responsibility of ensuring a company or organisation runs smoothly and is healthy (financially, culturally, etc.).

> Keep away from those who try to belittle your ambitions. Small people always do that, but the really great ones make you believe that you, too, can become great.
>
> – MARK TWAIN

The difference between your BOD and inner sanctum is that the inner sanctum is comprised of the people you're closest to – your friends and family. They are the ones you turn to for help with personal dilemmas. Whereas the BOD are usually purely focused on helping you navigate your career.

Board of directors v mentoring

Mentoring can be a powerful career strategy as well, but we prefer boards to mentors for the following reasons:

▲ Asking someone to be your mentor (one person rather than a group of people) can be a scary proposition for time-poor people. While they might want to be of assistance to you, they may be more willing to help if they know you are not reliant on just them. By spreading the load, not only do you make it easier on your board, you are the beneficiary of diverse experiences and opinions. You also grow your network and your potential capacity to connect with your BOD's networks.

▲ Mentoring is becoming outdated. Your needs will change over time, so it's smarter to have a group of people to turn to, rather than relying on one person.

▲ Women are, by and large, mentored to death and, arguably, it hasn't improved things much for them (it certainly hasn't had any effect on the numbers of women holding senior positions). A better approach is needed than straight mentoring. Women need advocates, people who can open doors or push their names forward when it counts. Women need a group of people that they can regularly consult with and get feedback from. A team is much more powerful than an individual.

What the BOD helps you avoid

Having a personal board of directors prevents you from being short-sighted. People have a tendency to pay attention to data that supports their conclusions and ignore information that doesn't (the technical term for this is confirmation bias). In other words, we seek out information that validates our views and beliefs. And the more strongly held our opinions or beliefs, the more likely we are to ignore data that may challenge our position. Having a BOD means having people around you who can hold you accountable and open your mind to different information and new ways of thinking.

The best way to ensure you are making great decisions is to surround yourself with diversity, and we are not just talking gender. A variety of life experiences, ages, industries and perspectives will give you the opportunity to be challenged, supported and may build your confidence and add to your performance. But surrounding ourselves with different types of people is not our default position. In general, we put people around us that look like us and value the same things. Actively seeking out other styles and types of people for your BOD should be deliberate, and can greatly strengthen your position.

Who is on your board?

Some people will already be there by default. Think of a big life decision you might face, such as deciding to take a new job or moving overseas – the fork in the road type decisions. Who do you turn to at these times? Whose judgement do you trust? These people will naturally already have a place on your board.

RULES FOR CREATING YOUR BOARD OF DIRECTORS

1. SELECT 'TIGERS' AS WELL AS CHEERLEADERS

There is no point having only cheerleaders on your board – your mates and others who only ever see the positives and want to celebrate your success. While you want people around to do this, you also need at least a few who can give you constructive feedback, challenge you or deliver the hard truth when it's needed. Choose a couple of tigers to give you a different perspective.

Other qualities that potential board members might have include:

- **Good values**
  Everyone needs 'value guards' – people who will sound the alarm if they see you losing sight of your values and integrity. When you are under pressure or feeling stressed or anxious, it can be easy to slide into bad habits without noticing you've changed direction.

- **Perspective**
  Choose people who are willing to share their experiences with you, but stop short of making decisions for you. Some people simply cannot see their own biases when it comes to dishing out advice.

2. TEACH YOUR BOARD HOW TO WORK FOR YOU BY INVESTING IN THEM

You must guide your BOD in how you want them to work for you. Regularly spending time with them (including virtual or phone time) is important to cultivate the relationship. Expecting them to do the work is not what it's about. *You* must drive the relationship and the agenda.

3. THINK ACROSS AND DOWN, NOT JUST UP

It is normal for people to choose people they look up to as their board members. But you are just as likely to learn from those around you. Think about including a mix of generations as well. For example, we know that as women in our mid- to late thirties, we might not know it all when it comes to masterfully using social media for our business. By getting younger, savvy twenty-somethings in our corner, we stand the best chance of being ahead of the curve, rather than simply keeping up.

4. AIM FOR AN ODD NUMBER OF BOARD MEMBERS

The optimal number of board members is five. Why? Because you can't hope to maintain a strong connection with many more, and it works to have an odd number – that way, if you are ever facing a decision that you want to consult all board members about, you will have an odd number of 'votes'. Having a tie would just confuse you even more.

Leigh's Story

Some examples of people I have sought out to be on my BOD:

- A person who has loads more experience than me in my industry and has helped me navigate some of the gender issues I have encountered.

- A Chair of a board (a real one!) that I love to observe in action. I admire how she goes about things and aspire to develop my skill set in the same way.

- A colleague who has a knack for telling it how it is. I can always rely on them to give me the real picture, warts and all (yes, it's sometimes hard to hear, but is essential for my development).

- A leader who always gives me something to think about, and who is happy to share their stories of success and failure, which has given me so many learning opportunities.

- Someone who always pumps me up and is hugely supportive. I go to this person when I'm feeling a bit flat or need some reassurance. (But I don't go to them when I want the real picture – that is not a strong point.)

I really feel that having a Board of Directors has been my secret career weapon. The power of having smart, experienced, thoughtful people adding value to my thoughts and decisions has been incredible, particularly at times where I have been at a crossroad (personally and professionally). And what's more, it's a fairly cost-neutral exercise (all it has ever cost me is a few coffees and lunches). I have learnt that your board members get as much out of it as you do. Great people help others to be great, it's simple.

Early on in my career, I always made sure I had a mentor. These were such positive experiences, but I was always a bit worried about having just one person in my corner. I didn't want them to feel like helping me was a responsibility or chore.

So I created my own BOD. 'Membership' of my board changes over time, as I meet new people or think that I need something different depending on what I'm doing in my career. I have tried to create as diverse a group as possible, and I always have an odd number.

be your best self

Start to create your own BOD, using the following prompter questions to help you choose the best people.

- Vision and motivation: Who inspires you? Who is known for taking action? Who always has fresh ideas?

- Personal development: Who makes you a better you? Who is able to give you constructive and useful feedback? Who is not afraid to challenge you? Who pushes you to consider things differently?

- Personal support: Who can get you back on track quickly? Who are you able to debrief with? Who can you be yourself around? Who gives you great encouragement and support, and genuinely wants to be there for you?

- Wellbeing: Who encourages your health (mental and physical)? Who helps you learn and grow as a person? Who helps you strengthen your relationships, and your connection to the community?

- Knowledge and expertise: Who can build your knowledge in the areas you want to explore? Who has 'been there, done that' and is willing to share their advice and experience? Who do you respect professionally? Who could connect you to others in the area?

WINNING PLAYS

- A PERSONAL BOD IS A POWERFUL CAREER TOOL TO HELP YOU AVOID CONFIRMATION BIAS.

- SELECTING A DIVERSE RANGE OF PEOPLE FOR YOUR BOD IS IMPORTANT. DON'T JUST SELECT CHEERLEADERS IF YOU ARE SERIOUS ABOUT SUCCESS.

- IF YOU GO TO THE TROUBLE OF CREATING A BOD, YOU NEED TO MAKE SURE YOU NURTURE IT. GIVE BACK AS MUCH AS YOU CAN.

CHAPTER 15
GET AHEAD OF THE GAME

I can.

I will.

END OF STORY.

Keeping one step ahead requires a strategy. Attaining and sustaining your best self means you have to stay focused and on track. This sounds like hard work, but it doesn't have to be – preparing for different scenarios means that when inevitable challenges flood in, they don't swallow you up and wash your aspirations away in the current.

Cook up the following to give your performance an edge: 2 parts determination, 1 part expect the unexpected, 3 parts push the boundaries and then wash it down with a tall glass of grace under pressure ... voila!

DETERMINATION

One of the things we love to do is celebrate all of the successful women we know personally or admire from afar. We created a feature called *Success Stripped Back* on our website (www.theignitionproject.com.au) because we wanted to showcase real, honest and raw stories that never get told. One thing that stands out in all of these amazing women is how determined they are to get what they want.

Talent certainly plays a part, and maybe initially that's what helped them find their passion, but sheer determination seems to be the major contributing factor, especially when you hear that what they wanted was harder to get than they ever imagined. But they all dare to be different; they have huge amounts of courage to do things that no-one has done before. It's like they are all adrenaline junkies trying to get their fix. Some people do that by jumping out of planes, others set themselves crazy—amazing goals that might take years to achieve but they do it, believe it and work hard enough to get exactly what they wanted and more.

Determined people share:

Passion

Discipline

Willpower

Ambition

Finding a balance of the attributes above is a crucial part of the recipe. Too much of one can disrupt the others, and sometimes you will feel that just one of them is your driving force.

How to maintain determination for the long haul:

▲ Be selfish. A determined attitude includes the ability to think independently; know your values and stick to them. Don't listen to anyone who says the sacrifices are not worth it or you should do less. Perhaps they are doing too little? Athletes know there are things they need to do that may not fit in with other people's views (for example, training often, going to bed early, staying away from alcohol), but they do it anyway.

▲ View obstacles as speed bumps rather than showstoppers. Take whatever steps you have to, to move through or around the obstacle. Remaining determined through the inevitable ups and downs is about maintaining your positivity and focus. Make lemonade from lemons.

▲ Make the most of the time you have. Don't procrastinate; just do the next thing you need to do to move towards reaching your goals. Get organised and declutter your diary and surroundings. You will be more determined if you don't waste time.

▲ Remind yourself of the end game often. Don't make it all about the work. Dream about the end point and how it will feel to get there. Remind yourself of what you are working towards and why it is worth it as often as possible.

The mentally challenging side of sport is the bit no-one else can see, so it's hard to really tell if a teammate is coping with all of the demands that are placed upon them. This goes for anyone in any job, for that matter.

When it came to netball, I loved being under pressure in a game; I loved when people doubted my ability and when everything was against me. You always know your strengths and your weaknesses; I knew I wasn't physically gifted, aside from my height, but that one of my strengths was my mental toughness.

I was most mentally tested at the end of my career. You don't realise what an isolating experience being an athlete in a team sport can be until you are in rehab or getting old, as I was. I could no longer do any sort of training without doing recovery alongside it. It meant long hours on the massage table (not as pleasant as it sounds), in the pool, stretching, or simply just lying down so my body wouldn't hurt.

The rest of the team would all leave training and go home while I headed to Carlton Football Club on my own to swim in the pool and sit in the ice bath in the hope it would help me pull up better the next day. I didn't mind putting in the extra hours, but I hated how lonely I felt having to do so much more than anyone else, just to play a game of netball. At our 6 am weights

Bianca's Story

sessions I would hardly be able to move, my joints were nowhere near warm enough to lift or jump. Getting off a plane and straight to training was almost impossible but I needed and wanted to do everything with the team. I really struggled to overcome the constant feeling of isolation and not knowing how much more I could push my body before it broke down completely.

I had never had to deal with anything like that before; I've always been able to find a solution to fix whatever was wrong. Retirement was my eventual solution, but I still loved playing and wanted to make sure my final year was an enjoyable one.

As captain, I always tried to be a positive influence on the girls and it took all of my energy to hide how I was really feeling. All the medical staff and support staff would be as empathetic as they possibly could but I didn't want to be a drain on the team.

So how do you cope when you really aren't coping? You make some changes!

I had to change the way I was thinking about it all. If every time I went to Carlton for recovery I was in a bad mood or feeling sorry for myself, then it was going to get harder and harder.

I had to make being in the ice bath somewhat fun, so I'd put my music on and distract myself. Some of the girls started to come with me, which stopped me stressing or thinking about my body as much, and made it far more entertaining. I'd organise dinner with friends afterwards so I had something to look forward to. And I reminded myself a million times about enjoying every moment of that year. I forced myself to think of one thing that I loved after every training session (no matter how hard it was).

I was selective in who I surrounded myself with; I spent as much time as I could with the younger girls. Their positive energy and enthusiasm was contagious to the point that I acted like I was 18 most of the season. Their vibe changed mine and made me stop wasting my energy worrying about myself.

While doing all this didn't completely fix the pain I was in, it provided me with a distraction, a way to cope and a way to get through it.

I loved my final year – my body didn't. But making some decisions early on to change the way I was processing it certainly made it a lot easier. Where there's a will, there's a way!

EXPECT THE UNEXPECTED

How can we possibly expect the unexpected if we don't expect it to happen? Let's keep it simple: if you are aware and open to change, you will be able to handle whatever comes your way with calmness and grace. That's the ideal anyway. As an added bonus, being prepared is also a great stress and anxiety buster.

Athletes spend their whole professional lives preparing and training their bodies to be able to cope with the demands of their sport. They also spend a considerable amount of time mentally preparing themselves to ensure they can handle the pressure, stress and nerves when it comes to game time. Yet they can't possibly prepare and plan for everything. Things happen. Injuries happen. The best thing they can do is to step back and be aware of their thoughts and reactions; adopt a calm approach to dealing with the issue; change tack, and take the next step forward.

When we're formulating a plan, we spend a huge amount of time creating plan A, but it's just as important to make sure that we also dedicate time to our contingency plans. Make sure there is a plan B and, if you are super organised and want to cover all bases, maybe even a plan C and D.

There will be times when the unexpected occurs and it's impossible to plan for it or cope with it, at least initially. It will take all your time and resources to cope. The main aim during hard times like this is to try and get your stress levels under control whenever you feel ready to do so. Afterwards, take some time out to reflect, refresh and revitalise your mind and body.

PUSH THE BOUNDARIES

By now you're probably aware we're all for you empowering yourself, taking control of your life, acting like a boss and owning it. The more you own it, the better, right?

Yes, but with a big caveat.

You still need to put yourself in uncomfortable or stressful situations.

If you always take the easy option or the comfortable one, you will only ever be the same – you won't grow or change or evolve. Your mind will get lazy if it's never challenged or put under pressure.

The boundaries we set are there to be tested, stretched, pushed and broken. Don't ignore them. Don't accept them. If you want success, real success, you need to start doing things differently. Embrace your curiosity; allow it to guide you, and you will always find something new. And, chances are, you will never be bored in the process.

GRACE UNDER PRESSURE

Where there is a lot of pressure, a graceful person retains their usual calm manner. Pressure pushes us and places demands on our physical, mental and emotional wellbeing and this can feel, well, less than ideal. But don't forget, we have the power to control the decisions we make. By choosing to remain calm under pressure, you can transform a not ideal situation into something that builds your brand. Practise making better decisions (because you are not in panic mode) that reflect your true values and might even be able to reduce any damage that may have occurred. Showing grace during the times you really want to do the opposite is not easy, but it points to your true character and builds resilience for the long term.

We've mentioned the power of a positive mindset; it can help in pressured situations too. Trusting in your preparations, your plan and your ability to push through the roadblocks to get the result you want is part of the positive mindset equation.

Courage is grace under pressure.
– ERNEST HEMINGWAY

Visualisation is a tool used by athletes to help them deal with the stress of an impending big game or selections. The process involves you mentally rehearsing the movements you need to do to reach that successful outcome, how you will look doing it, how you will feel in the moment, and all the possible outcomes that could unfold. It's a powerful tool and is definitely not just for athletes. Everyone can do it and enjoy the benefits. The best part is that visualising success isn't particularly difficult or time consuming, you can do it anywhere at anytime and can do it for as long as you like. You'll be surprised at the power of visualisation when things evolve exactly as you saw it.

Seeing is believing

It's always inspiring to watch athletes achieve incredible feats. Cathy Freeman winning gold at the Sydney Olympics, with the weight of the world on her shoulders, was the epitome of performing under pressure. In every interview she did, fascinatingly, she described running as, 'her place of serenity'.

'The pressure coming from the media or the country, kind of absolutely paled into insignificance compared to what I was expecting myself. So ten years lead up to this one moment, not much could have happened to set me off my course of destiny.' – Catherine Freeman

Steps to work through high-pressure situations:

▲ Be aware of the situation by acknowledging the stress, pressure and challenge ahead.

▲ Trust in your knowledge, skills and the plans you have in place.

▲ Visualise how you will navigate through it successfully and all the possible scenarios that could take place.

▲ Execute with calmness and grace.

▲ Feel the release once it's over (this part won't be easy, but it will be worth it).

be your best self

Close your eyes and think about a time when you have been under enormous pressure.

Think about how you felt, what you were thinking, how you looked, who was there and what you did.

Now write down your reflections.

In the future, what are three things you would do differently in this situation?

WINNING PLAYS

- DETERMINATION IS A SET OF LEARNED SKILLS, RATHER THAN SOMETHING YOU ARE BORN WITH. YOU CAN IMPLEMENT STRATEGIES TO INCREASE YOUR DETERMINATION FOR ANY SITUATION.

- PREPARATION IS THE KEY TO DEALING WITH WHATEVER COMES YOUR WAY. IF YOU HAVE A PLAN A, B AND C, YOU CAN PULL THEM FROM YOUR TOOLKIT WHENEVER YOU NEED TO AVOID STRESS AND MAKE A QUICK DECISION. YOU WILL HAVE ALREADY DONE THE HARD WORK.

- GRACE UNDER PRESSURE IS NEVER EASY, BUT KEEPS YOU CLOSER TO YOUR LONG-TERM GOALS THAN PANICKING OR HAVING A HISSY FIT. LEAVE THAT FOR THE TWO YEAR OLDS. PULL UP YOUR SOCKS AND USE GRACE TO GET YOU ON YOUR WAY.

... owning our story
and loving ourselves
through that process
is the bravest thing
that we will ever do.

– BRENÉ BROWN

The game plan

put it all together, get on your way

You're here. You have thought about what success really is for you, the potential mind games you play that get in your way, what kind of leader you want to become and built a toolkit to help you ignite your career and leadership path. Now, just before we leave you to get your game on, we are going to remind you of the importance of looking after yourself and inspire you to take action today. And then … drum roll, please … it's over to you. You'll then move on to building your game plan to be your best self. We are here for you, every step of the way. Let's do this.

Action always beats intention.

- JON ACUFF

CHAPTER 16
CHOOSE YOU

Our work in high-performance environments has taught us so much about what it takes to be the best you can be. And in sport as in life, being your best self means the difference between a successful result and a not so good one. If athletes are not at their peak, physically, mentally and spiritually (hang in there, we will explain), then their performance suffers. Talent is only part of the performance equation. To really nail your dreams, you need to work towards your best self. Every. Single. Day.

Being your best self is a mindset rather than a goal with an end point, which is one of the reasons people find it so hard to conceptualise. The journey towards this state is long, with lots of speed bumps. Is it worth it? Ask yourself, would you like to live and perform at your peak, so that you can get the best results possible? Would you like to have an impact on people and the things you are passionate about? Would you like to play big and live your own version of success?

Women in particular need to keep an eye on their physical and mental health ... We need to do a better job of putting ourselves higher on our own 'to do' list.

– MICHELLE OBAMA

We hope you answered, 'YES!' And before your mind races off, don't give one thought to the 'how' (at least not right now). Being your best self starts with committing to doing it. The 'how' often trips people up from even starting because their mind races to all the reasons they can't do it or it might be hard. So, don't get sucked in. Just stay in the moment, visualising your best self and what that might look like for you.

GET ON YOUR WAY

Let's get physical

Nothing awesome can happen without your health. How do you get from where you are now (point A), to where you want to be (point 'be')?

The only vehicle you have at your disposal is your body. Like your car, when it is maintained and properly loved, it gets you to where you want to go smoothly over the speed bumps and doesn't break down. If you are serious about nailing a career and life you love, you need a physical advantage.

There are a million excuses out there dressed up as reasons. You don't have to become a gym junkie or even join a gym. It doesn't have to cost money. You can get up out of your chair right now and JUST DO SOMETHING. You don't even need to know anything about exercise, as there are so many phone apps that will walk you through the specifics. Start seeing the benefits exercise offers and its positive impact on your performance, rather than wanting to change the things you don't like about your body.

Know yourself

If you really want to live your best version of you, then you need to be able to answer the question of who you really are. You have to know what your strengths and development opportunities are, and be aware of your mindset, habits and the things you are interested in. You then have all the data you need to work out what being your best self means for you. If you only have half the picture, you end up with a career and life that only resembles a bit of you — or worse — not at all. Understanding what you are working with is what you do when leading others; it is the same when you are trying to lead yourself.

Get happy

Happiness doesn't just happen. Figure out what makes you happy and do more of it. Life is too short to not do the things that bring you the most happiness. It's as simple as that.

You are your habits

This one is hard to make sound like a sexy tip that will have you rushing out to try it. However, if you are the sum of your habits, those habits will serve you better. Top performers are great at implementing the boring stuff, the things that no-one really sees, day in, day out. But this structure gives them a chance to be their best selves.

> I think self-awareness is probably the most important thing towards being a champion.
> – BILLIE JEAN KING

Establish a positive daily routine and stick to it. Do the things that work for you (for example, it might be getting up earlier so you can read, feed the soul, exercise, meditate, prepare for the day ahead), then just repeat them, over and over, until they are simply part of you and what you do.

Leigh's routine:

5.30–6 am: Get up, glug a glass of water, exercise. I have learned over the years that if I leave exercising to later in the day, it doesn't happen. And I have to not think about it otherwise the excuses creep in. Get up, get moving.

I have two versions of my day: either I'm in my home office working, or out with clients. So my working day begins anywhere from 8–9 am.

7–9 am: Get the kids up, feed and water them and myself (it's always the same breakfast – muesli with blueberries, often prepared the night before to save time in the morning), then I do the school run. This is the most insane time of the day in my house. I do what needs to be done (washing, chuck dinner in the slow cooker ready for later in the day, clean the shower while I'm in it, etc.) to help the day go smoother later on.

9–10 am: If I'm working in my home office, I will use the first hour to sort stuff – this means emails, bills, calls, a load of washing and a cup of tea.

10 am–12.30 pm: Emails are off, head down, bum up. Time to work.

12.30 pm: Lunch – I'm usually starving by then. Quick read of the paper, then I give our four-legged baby, Stella, some love.

1–2.30 pm: Check emails, make calls and do some work.

2.30–7 pm: School run, kids sports activities, dinner.

7–10 pm: Work. This is when I find I'm often most productive.

10.30 pm: Bed. I'm a night owl who has been retrained in the value of sleep. It's so important in getting through the day well! Dark room, no technology in the bedroom allowed. I even turn off the wi-fi so our bodies can get a complete rest from the technological energy that is present.

bianca's routine:

This was quite a difficult task for me. That sounds crazy, I know, because I led such a structured life as an athlete. After retiring, and taking on running my own businesses and living a very entrepreneurial lifestyle, I quickly realised that there is no normal day for me now. I love this most of the time, but other days I crave some normality.

Here is my attempt to show you an average day!

7 am: Wake up. I always set my alarm for 7; I don't like to waste the morning. First thing I do is check my phone, social media, etc. I like being up to date on what's happening in the news. I try and have some time out without my phone, so going for a 30-minute walk is important.

I love a green smoothie to start the day (kale, celery, lemon, spinach and berries) as well as some porridge. A good eating routine helps me keep the rest of my day in check.

8 am–12 pm: I'll either be catching up on emails or meeting with people. When I can, I try to schedule all my meetings in the morning so that my whole day isn't spent driving around. They usually take place in cafés, so green tea has become my drink of choice and my fave café meeting spots are determined by whether they have wi-fi or not!

Lunchtime: I'm always on the road and rarely at home, so I try and grab something healthy on the run.

1–5 pm: It's either more meetings setting up projects, or it's presenting a workshop or a speaking engagement at a school or business. I love doing this, but preparation is key.

5–7 pm: Usually gym time. I've found that my joints don't love exercising in the mornings (thanks netball) so finishing the day doing something active is one of my only constants. On my way home there is always a supermarket stop, as I don't plan dinner ahead very often.

7–10 pm: This is usually the only time I watch TV. It's either a good reality show (think *The Kardashians* … don't judge), news or sport related. I watch TV while getting prepared for the next day. I make sure I have done any presentations I need to do, read emails and am up to date.

I'm aware of how important getting a good night's sleep is, but I'm not sure I've really managed to consistently do this. I always aim for eight hours, so if I have an early start I'll be in bed a lot earlier, but on a normal day I'm in bed by 10.30 pm.

Feed the soul

Feeding your soul has such a big role to play in being the best person you can be. Nourishing your spirit tends to keep you motivated and forward thinking. If life becomes all work and no play, it feels too much like a slog.

What do you do that you really enjoy, just for fun? What does your downtime look like? In every elite team, the pressure is enormous. There are a lot of serious, task-focused things to get done every day and week. But this is always interspersed with a whole lot of fun and downtime. This recharges athletes' brains and bodies, and gets them ready for the next surge. It's the same with you. Make sure you are feeding your soul full-fat dinners, not just throwing it breadcrumbs from time to time.

Be in the moment

We both love watching the world's top sporting performers in action. Why? Because they are totally in the moment, and enjoying the experience for what it is. When athletes start to wander into thinking about the past or future, it affects what they are able to do in the present. We know logically that the present moment is all we have, but sometimes need to make the emotional and behavioural leap. As we have talked about (see p. 50), the practice of mindfulness can really help you to focus on the present.

Surround yourself with top people

Be unrelentingly scrupulous about who you let into your inner sanctum. If you really do become like the five people you spend most of your time with, those five need to be well chosen. Spend less time around the tyre-kickers and more time around people that inspire you. Even if those people can't be in your immediate inner sanctum, you can have them as part of your support team – think writers, Instagram accounts, bloggers, the magazines you read and the things you watch on TV. Filter the negativity and let the inspiring stuff in.

Giving and helping

Sport, from the grassroots to the elite, is full of volunteers. In fact without them, sport just wouldn't exist as we know it. It's the unpaid, behind-the-scenes jobs that never get the amount of recognition they ought to. Why do so many do it? Because it feels amazing to give back and be part of something bigger than yourself. While giving and helping might look different to you (it doesn't have to be sport, it could be anything), it nonetheless can have the same positive benefits. Integrate giving and helping into your career and life, because the truth is that it will help you be your best self much, much more than you realise.

Bianca's story

I pretty much thought I could do anything in my early 20s and that I'd be OK. I tried to keep up with my 'normal' friends and be social every night; I tried to be an elite athlete and push my body to the limit, because that was what I thought was going to make me the best. I failed miserably, many times over.

I got glandular fever at 24 and this ended up being the wake-up call I needed to remind me of how precious my body really was.

I remember looking in the mirror and seeing an incredibly pale person (paler than my normal pre-fake-tanned skin). My eyes were a greyish colour and I didn't even recognise who I was looking at. I thought to myself, *what is wrong with me?'*

After that, I went on a steep learning curve about what I needed to do to be kind to myself and not do everything in extremes. I had to change my diet dramatically (hence the green smoothies now) to provide my body with what it needed. If I wanted to be an elite athlete, I needed to rest, sleep, take time out for myself, be organised and find balance.

What I've learnt is that it doesn't always make sense to everyone around you, but you have to make some choices for you, not for anyone else.

It doesn't come naturally to me, but I've come a very long way. Every day now I consciously choose to make time to be kind to myself. It can be as simple as going for a walk, reading, spending time with family and friends, playing with my niece, taking out my stand-up paddle board or simply just sitting still. These are the things that I love doing and I know now I need to make time for them.

Review

Hey you with that never-ending list – stop what you are doing right now! You might be getting stuff done, and it might *feel* like the shortest way to your goal, but if you never give yourself a chance to process, reflect and adjust where you need to, you won't approach situations with new insights or perspectives.

Think of it this way, each business creates a strategic plan. They then come back to this plan, at regular intervals, to assess and re-evaluate, refining their strategy as they learn more. Reflection is an important business strategy. It's also an important personal strategy.

Give yourself a fighting chance to be the best you can be by incorporating the habit of review into your toolkit. Review doesn't need to be a complicated activity, but should be an opportunity to check in on what is working or needs rethinking.

You get the idea. You may have tried some of the strategies we've outlined before, but did you review? Did you look for ways to enhance what you have done previously? We are often so focused on doing and being busy that we forget that the review stage is super important. When you review, you move on to the next goal with confidence, rather than speeding through, doing more, but not necessarily doing better. Ask yourself, what went wrong? What went right? What would you do differently next time? What do you need to ditch? This way you are not just floating through life, but learning and developing from each experience and moving closer to being your best self. Build on what works, no matter how small or insignificant it may seem. You don't know where it may lead.

be your best self

Choose one of the things we have talked about in this chapter to change things up in your life right now. What is the one thing that will have impact today? Commit to doing something different each day for a week — plan, do, review, enhance.

WINNING PLAYS

- NOTHING GREAT CAN HAPPEN IF YOU AREN'T HEALTHY. PUT EFFORT INTO ATTAINING AND MAINTAINING YOUR HEALTH. IT'S NOT SELFISH, IT'S CRITICAL.

- SELF-AWARENESS IS KING.

- HABITS ARE WHO YOU ARE AND DETERMINE WHAT YOU ARE CAPABLE OF.

- FEED THE SOUL TO REJUVENATE, AND SO YOU ARE READY FOR THE NEXT PERIOD OF INTENSITY.

- KEEP YOUR PLANS SIMPLE. YOU ARE MORE LIKELY TO STICK TO THEM.

CHAPTER 17
MAKE THINGS HAPPEN

The game of life has two participants - spectators and players.
Pick one.

– ANONYMOUS

A big part of being successful is to at some point (sooner rather than later), stop banging on and start making it all happen. Some people are very good at planning - so good in fact that they stay in the planning phase for much longer than they need to. While having a nice, shiny plan might look great, substance is what we are after. Nothing happens unless you DO SOMETHING. The aim here is to not let perfection stand in the way of good - don't wait for the perfect day, the perfect vision board or the perfect moment. Get out of your own way and make great things happen. The time to do it is now.

CALLING IT OUT

Do you need to call yourself in any of the following areas?

False assumptions

Often we look to attach past successes or failures to present-day events. For example, if something has failed before, we automatically think it will fail again. This is not always the case! Just because something has happened before, doesn't mean it will happen again — the past does not predict your future. Believing that things are certain impacts your behaviour.

> Your assumptions are your windows on the world. Scrub them off every once in a while, or the light won't come in.
>
> – ISAAC ASIMOV

Dressing excuses up as reasons

We bet you hear excuses dressed up as reasons all the time, but have you checked yours? What are your justifications for playing small and are they really valid? The primary role of a dressed up excuse is to lessen your responsibility load (at least in your own head). Running away from your owning your reasons isn't going to change your game anytime soon. What's your favourite excuse? Our favourite is, 'I'm so busy'. Busy is the new four-letter word, and using it as an excuse enables you to avoid taking full responsibility for what you prioritise. **If you want it, you will find a way. If you don't, you will find an excuse.**

Thinking the little things don't matter

Do you sometimes convince yourself that the little things don't matter; or that 'just this once' doesn't count? As we've discussed, habits make up our character, so if your habits don't support your version of success, they need to be changed. Little things should be relabelled 'little big things' to keep you honest about how much seemingly small things matter. Add all the small things up over time to really see the impact.

Saying, 'I don't know how she does it'

Using this phrase lets you off the hook. You *do* know how she does it — hard work, persistence, a great plan and support from her inner sanctum. There is no secret. If you don't want to do the work, don't do it. But don't delude yourself that others are better than you.

Using talk to avoid action

Some people are very good at doing a lot of talking but not taking much action. Action, even a small step, triumphs talk every time. If you want to make things happen, you have to do something. Call yourself on what's really going on. Maybe you are fearful, anxious or worried. Label it so you can work through it.

Blaming others or things

The blame game is not the game you want to be playing. It's always easier to blame others or things and much harder to accept our own role when things aren't going well. By becoming the judge, jury and executioner of others, you miss a critical opportunity to learn more and adjust your success strategy as you go.

MAKING IT
HAPPEN HABITS

1. SAY YES AND FIGURE OUT THE HOW LATER.

Take on new opportunities and use them to grow your skills. Take chances.

2. PAY ATTENTION. START TO NOTICE WHAT IS HAPPENING AROUND YOU.

Focus on what behaviours and skills of yours are valued by others. Notice the impact you have and how you might leverage that into even more adventures.

3. BELIEVE IN YOURSELF. BELIEVE IN THE THINGS YOU DO.

Make time to build confidence, as it doesn't just happen.

4. BE DECISIVE.

Don't let opportunities pass by because you can't make a decision. Decide what you want to accomplish. Make plans, set goals. Being decisive means working out what you want from life and what you are willing to do to achieve it.

5. DON'T WAIT TO BE MOTIVATED.

People with good habits are not always one hundred per cent motivated to do them. You don't need to be motivated – you just need to get it done.

be your best self

Many people just wait on the sidelines, hoping they might get a tap on the shoulder or an opportunity. You need to take action and jump in with both feet. **Be bold.** What needs your attention and action? Put the book down right now and go and do one thing that you know you have been putting off.

WINNING PLAYS

- YOU CAN TALK ABOUT IT ALL YOU WANT, BUT ACTION IS WHAT IS NEEDED. SOMETIMES THE BEST THING YOU CAN DO FOR YOURSELF IS TO GET OUT OF YOUR OWN WAY!

- JUSTIFYING PLAYING SMALL IS EASY. CHANGING IT FOR YOURSELF IS MORE DIFFICULT, BUT WORTH IT. TAKE THE HIGH ROAD.

- BEING YOUR BEST SELF MEANS CALLING YOURSELF OUT.

#NAILINGIT

Strategies to try right now:

- ▲ **Avoid endless polishing.** Don't let perfect stand in the way of good.

- ▲ **Keep it simple.** Focus simply on the next action that needs to be done, even when you feel like there is so much in front of you. In one line, describe what you need to do to get that thing done. Then work on the next action in front of you, rather than all the steps beyond that.

- ▲ **Have compassion for the most important person. You.** It's often easier to give it away than to give it to ourselves. Success is a journey that requires you to be good and kind to yourself, just as you would be to a friend. It's OK to have bad days and meltdowns – just don't unpack and set up camp there.

- ▲ **Get comfortable with being uncomfortable.** Achieving what you want to achieve will require you to get out of your comfort zone – past the fear and amongst the tough stuff.

- ▲ **Stop questioning your ability.** Don't undervalue what you are and overvalue what you aren't. The real question is, how much of your ability are you prepared to use?

- ▲ **Do what others are not prepared to do.** Most people want to know where the shortcut is. They won't persist. An easy way to succeed is to do what others will not. Different results = doing things a different way.

- ▲ **Focus on everyday habits.** The sum of these is your performance. What helps and what holds you back? Cultivate habits that look after your wellbeing so you can go the distance.

▲ **Aim for personal excellence, the rest will take care of itself.** The only person you are competing against is you. Work on what you can control and let the rest flow.

▲ **Trust yourself.** Trust in your skills and capacity to learn, even in the face of the tyre-kickers. They will always be there – how much space you give them in your head is up to you. You are the landlord of your life!

▲ **Do something your future self will thank you for rather than worrying about your past self.** Track records do not have to predict future success. That's entirely up to you, and what you choose to do today and beyond.

▲ **Go for tiny adjustments that add up over time.** Rather than big changes that are hard to sustain, change small things to move you towards your version of success.

▲ **Play the games that matter, not the useless mind games that get you nowhere.** Give them up to be healthier and happier.

▲ **Be grateful for what you have, where you have come from and the things you have learned.** Demonstrate gratefulness by being your best self, honouring your unique talents, skills and the contribution you can make.

YOUR HIGH-PERFORMANCE GAME PLAN

BRINGING IT ALL TOGETHER

Formulating your game plan is not a difficult process, particularly if you have been reflecting on each chapter as you read the book. There is also not a right or wrong way to do it – it depends on your style (for example, Bianca likes to use the computer for this type of work, whereas Leigh loves to get the butcher's paper out and brainstorm). The act of writing forces you to slow down, reflect and think deeply. Writing has proven health benefits (positively affecting stress levels), and also engages both sides of your brain, so you are bound to encounter new feelings and come up with new solutions or aspirations. The way you do it is not the most important thing – doing it is! So find what works for you.

Spend some time on this; don't answer the questions like they are a shopping list. Make sure you are listening to your own voice and being as honest with yourself as possible. Go somewhere that inspires you and take the time you need.

Getting your game on

▲ What is the vision for your life?

▲ Is it your vision, or someone else's?

▲ What kind of mindset do you currently have?

▲ What habits are holding you back?

▲ People you are grateful for …

▲ Things you are grateful for …

▲ Experiences you are grateful for …

▲ What could you be happy about if you chose to be?

▲ Who is in your inner sanctum? How do you use them for success?

▲ How does emotional fitness play a role in your life — what needs attention?

▲ What is your most important relationship like (the one you have with yourself)?

Mind games

▲ How do you let fear keep you from being your best self?

▲ Who are the tyre-kickers in your life and who are your cheerleaders?

▲ What rules do you have that are getting in the way?

▲ Whose opinion do you really care about?

Take the lead

▲ What are your leadership beliefs?

▲ Do you really believe in yourself as a leader?

▲ What are your leadership values?

▲ Where are the opportunities to lead for you (professionally and personally)?

▲ What are your team skills? What do you want to develop?

You've got this

▲ What are your values? They become the filters by which you build and protect your brand. Choose three to five that are important to you, understanding that you can use values to help define what your version of success is.

▲ What do you really care about?

▲ What do you love doing?

▲ What are some aspirations that you have thought about, but not said out loud?

▲ If you could only do one thing for the rest of your life, what would it be?

▲ How do you deal with the unexpected, the confronting or the scary?

▲ What are you pretending not to know (about yourself, others or work situations)?

Game on!

▲ What does being your best self mean to you?

▲ What are your strengths?

▲ What are your talents?

▲ How might you need to get out of your own way?

▲ What will make the biggest difference to your success journey – what is your game changer?

▲ What will you need to give up to achieve your version of success?

▲ What is one thing you can do today that will matter tomorrow?

▲ What do you need to stop, start and keep to get your game on?

Why not you? Why not now?

Dear #GameOn woman,

So, you are here. The conclusion. But don't be fooled. This is like the fourth quarter of a game – what you do now counts more than ever. You are at an important juncture. So, what will you do? When you put this book down, you will have choices, just as you did before you started reading. This book can be just a good read, with a few tips and tricks, or it can serve as the catalyst for you doing things differently to get a different result.

We have one big question for you: what are you going to do to get your game on?

Channel your inner athlete. It might not be an aspiration of yours to ever be an athlete, but we can call upon the one that dwells within us all to help us navigate the challenges and choices we have. Our inner athlete is determined, resilient, inspired, assembles a great team around her and finds the courage to attain and sustain high levels of performance. Sometimes she doesn't want to go to training. Sometimes she finds it hard to get out of bed. But she shows up, and keeps showing up. She keeps her eye on the end game – being the best she can possibly be – which helps her get through the tough stuff. The skills you see athletes display in sporting arenas are in each one of us. They are not skills reserved for a special few. You have them on board now – it's a choice to develop and use them.

Do you remember that person who gave up? Neither does anyone else. Showing up is half the battle.

Don't wait – just do! Action is the most powerful thing that can overcome fear, anxiety and inertia. Action moves you forward, and helps to build the confidence and courage you might be waiting for. People talk a lot about building confidence and then doing what they really want to do. It doesn't work like that – confidence is built by action. Momentum is generated by a series of moments in a game, not isolated, one-off events. Stop being a passenger and get in the driver's seat. Get your game face on and do something.

Be your biggest fan. Stop treating yourself like the opposition. Stop your inner critic bad-mouthing you. We know what happens when fans get behind competitors – encouragement and support are far more potent than criticism and put-downs. Humans thrive on care and compassion. So do for yourself what you would do for others. Be gentle. Celebrate your steps forward, and not just the audacious ones.

And finally – wise up to what success really is. The next time you see #shinysuccess, don't get sucked in. A savvy woman like you knows that lots of factors contribute to a successful life and career. Play to your strengths and have a plan of attack for your RFIs (room for improvements). Deliberately put people in your inner sanctum that will help you, not drain you.

Time to play the game that matters! You know what to do, so get it together and go do it. We will be here, should you need to check in with us from time to time, on the sidelines, cheering you on.

Let's do this.

B & L x

> Above all, be the heroine of your own life, not the victim.
>
> – NORA EPHRON

THE IGNITION PROJECT

theignitionproject.com.au

This is how it all started for us. After hours of café catch-ups, phone calls and emails, we knew we needed to start a business to inspire women to connect, support and educate each other. We wanted women to share their real, stripped-back stories of success, and inspire one another to be the best they could be.

The Ignition Project was born — an online leadership and personal development e-course designed to give women and girls a toolkit for pursuing the life and career they want, based around practical information and strategies developed from our combined 30+ years of working with people in high-performance environments.

The Ignition Project (and the sister program, #youngchicks) speaks frankly about the challenges faced by the modern-day woman, including encounters in her career, building a personal brand, confidence and resilience, working through fear, and dealing with her inner critic.

Bianca Chatfield (@biancachatfield) Director, recently retired elite netballer, former netball captain, keynote speaker, leadership specialist, ambassador, teacher, media talent, broadcaster and columnist for the *Herald Sun*.

Bianca is one of the youngest players ever to have debuted for the Australian Diamonds, at the age of only 18. She made a name for herself on the court as one of the toughest defenders in the country, and as one of the most respected leaders in women's sport.

Leigh Russell (@leighmrussell) Leadership specialist, board director, performance coach, public speaker and facilitator. Leigh has qualifications in the arts, teaching, counselling, career counselling and business, and is the Mind Coach on Foxtel's *The Recruit*.

Leigh has worked with top athletes, coaches and administrators in elite sport across Australia. She has been a CEO, teacher and counsellor — experience that comes in handy when she walks through the door at night and transforms into her role as mother to three.

REFERENCES

[1] Korb, A 2012, *The Grateful Brain*. Available from: https://www.psychologytoday.com/blog/prefrontal-nudity/201211/the-grateful-brain

[2] Jabr, F 2013, *Why your brain needs more downtime*. Available from: http://www.scientificamerican.com/article/mental-downtime

[3] Brandt, M 2011, *Snooze you win? It's true for achieving hoop dreams, says study*. Available from: https://med.stanford.edu/news/all-news/2011/07/snooze-you-win-its-true-for-achieving-hoop-dreams-says-study.html

[4] The Black Dog Institute 2011, *Exercise and Depression*. Available from: http://www.blackdoginstitute.org.au/docs/ExerciseandDepression.pdf

[5] *What is Smiling Mind?* Available from: http://smilingmind.com.au/blog/#!/category/background/what-is-smiling-mind

[6] Adapted from Mohr, T 2014, *Playing Big: Find your voice, your vision and make things happen*, Hutchinson, New York.

[7] LeVan, A 2009, *Seeing Is Believing: The Power of Visualization*. Available from: https://www.psychologytoday.com/blog/flourish/200912/seeing-is-believing-the-power-of-visualization

[8] Wargo, E 2006, *How Many Seconds to a First Impression?* Available from: http://www.psychologicalscience.org/index.php/publications/observer/2006/july-06/how-many-seconds-to-a-first-impression.html

[9] Fey, T 2012, *Bossypants*, Little, Brown, New York.

ACKNOWLEDGEMENTS

We are grateful for ...

Chris Giannopoulos and the Bravo team for making this happen.

The team at Hardie Grant, especially Pam Brewster and Fran Berry, for believing in us, sharing our vision and helping us bring one of our dreams to fruition.

Our rock star editors, Rachel Day and Andrea O'Connor. Thank you for helping pull the ideas out of our heads, supporting and steering us through the whole process.

Design dynamo, Astred Hicks, who brought our book to life in such a beautiful way.

Our respective Boards of Directors. We are so grateful to be surrounded by so many super-talented, savvy people who are incredibly generous with their expertise and time.

The world of sport for all the lessons it has taught us (on and off the court), the people we have met, the places we have seen and the crazy experiences along the way. What a ride.

The women and girls who have completed The Ignition Project, who inspired us to delve deeper and write a book. We are grateful for your trust and feedback. We hope we have made an impact.

Leigh is especially grateful for ...

My support team who allowed me time to think and write around the craziness of children and the challenge of a deadline: my mum, my husband, my friends.

My amazing friend, business partner and fellow idea igniter, Bianca.

Bianca is especially grateful for ...

My family and friends who always support me whatever I'm doing, even though I'm sure they all think I'm crazy for taking the risks I do.

All of the teammates, coaches and support staff who have taught me so much and looked after me over the years.

Netball Australia and Netball Victoria for the opportunity to play netball.

And Leigh, who has become a great friend and is forever challenging, supporting and dreaming big for me like no other.

Published in 2016 by Hardie Grant Books

Hardie Grant Books (Australia)
Ground Floor, Building 1
658 Church Street
Richmond, Victoria 3121
www.hardiegrant.com.au

Hardie Grant Books (UK)
5th & 6th Floors
52–54 Southwark Street
London SE1 1UN
www.hardiegrant.co.uk

A Cataloguing-in-Publication entry is available from the catalogue of the National Library of Australia at www.nla.gov.au
Game On
ISBN 978 1 74379 183 7

Publisher: Fran Berry
Project Editor: Andrea O'Connor
Editor: Rachel Day
Designer: Astred Hicks
Photographer: Richard MacDonald
Production Manager: Todd Rechner

Colour reproduction by Splitting Image Colour Studio. Printed in China by 1010 Printing International Limited.

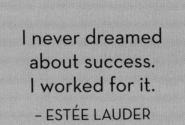

I never dreamed
about success.
I worked for it.

– ESTÉE LAUDER